# But God

# But God

SOMETIMES PURPOSE IS FOUND
IN YOUR DARKEST HOUR

*Nadine A. Raphael*

ISBN: 0692987398
ISBN 13: 9780692987391

*This book is dedicated to the many trials and valleys that I have experienced in life. To those trials that were meant to defeat me, destroy me, and even kill me: you failed! However, I thank you for visiting me, because without you, I wouldn't be the person that I am today. This book was birthed because of you. Thank You!*

# Contents

# Acknowledgments

I WOULD LIKE TO ACKNOWLEDGE my husband and best friend, Bentz. Thank you for embracing my many scars and flaws. Your love for me is a tangible demonstration of God's love for me and intentional plans for my life. To my three kids, Tenae, Isaiah, and Natacia, thank you for sacrificially allowing me to use my scars, my stories, and innumerable hours to help others. You are the real heroes!

To my mother, sister, and brother, we've been through a lot, but we're still standing! If I had to do this life all over again, I wouldn't want another family to do it with. I love you beyond words.

To my stepfather, Claude, thank you for always being consistently present.

To my Lord and Savior, thank you for giving me beauty in place of my ashes. The life you've given me, I now give back to you—fully yielded.

# Introduction

WHENEVER WE SEE "BUT GOD..." in the Bible, it often means God's intervention in a hopeless situation. God hijacks a negative circumstance and turns it around for the better. The book of Genesis tells us Joseph's brothers stripped him of his coat and threw him into a pit. Joseph's older brother, Reuben, persuaded the other brothers to throw Joseph into a cistern instead of killing him (intending to return later and pull Joseph out), but when Reuben was not there, Judah suggested they pull Joseph up and sell him to slave traders. After Joseph was sold to slave traders, the slave traders then sold him on an auction block as a slave. While Joseph was a slave in Egypt, he was falsely accused of attempted rape and thrown into prison. End of story, right? Wrong.

Joseph's brothers meant to cause him harm—to destroy his life. In their eyes, selling him to the traders made him as good as dead.

*But God intended it for good…*

Usually, whatever follows the words "But God…" cancels what preceded them. Those words herald a change in the trajectory of a person's life or a shift in a situation.

After years of enslavement and imprisonment, God elevated Joseph to prime minister—the second in command over Egypt, the nation he was once a slave to. Shortly after this miraculous positioning, Joseph's brothers traveled to Egypt looking for food during a great famine. However, what they found was something they wouldn't believe had they not seen it with their own eyes: the brother they sold into slavery many years before, the brother they thought was as good as dead, was now the leader of the nation where they were seeking help. Joseph's response to his treacherous brothers would be the platform upon which God's purpose and destiny for Joseph would be established. In Genesis 50:20 (New International Version), Joseph said to his brothers, "You intended to harm me, but God intended it for good to accomplish what is now being done, the saving of many lives."

This book is written on the foundation of those words. God has used the very thing meant to destroy my life to propel it. What Joseph's brothers did to destroy him was the first in events that God used to promote him. I am a living testimony that not only can God protect you in the middle of trials, but He can also promote you because of them.

> *Your destiny is chosen by God, but it's*
> *fulfillment is decided by you.*

—Dr. Myles Munroe

# CHAPTER 1

# A Sharp Right

*Hardships do not prevent you from your calling;*
*they prepare you for it. Sometimes the preparation*
*comes as a gift disguised as a painful blow!*

IN 1995 MY LIFE TOOK an unexpected sharp right turn. It was a brisk November morning in the suburbs of Virginia. Even though the sun was making attempts to shine, the clouds on that chilly morning muffled the beauty of the sun's rays.

It was about 7:30 a.m., but I could barely make it out of bed. I guess you would call it two months of morning sickness. Before I could reach the phone to call my fiancé to see what was taking him so long to return from the local 7-Eleven, the phone rang. For some reason, I felt an intense knot in my stomach when the phone rang, but I quickly reasoned that it was the discomfort of the morning sickness I had been experiencing.

On the other end of the phone was Paula, a family member of my fiancé, crying hysterically. "What's the matter?" I asked, fearing her response.

"They took my daughter, Nadine! Oh God, they have her! Please come get us!"

I could barely understand what she was saying through her uncontrollable sobbing. However, I could make out enough to understand that the police SWAT team, toting machine guns, had just searched her home with the aid of detection dogs, and they had arrested both her daughter and my fiancé. The content of that three-minute phone call dried all the saliva in my mouth; I tried to swallow but couldn't. I felt frozen with shock, but there was no time to sit and process.

The thump of the house phone on the floor, when it dropped from my hand, sounded no louder than the heartbeats pounding in my chest. I crawled out of the bed, my pregnant body not wanting to cooperate, and went to my two-year-old daughter's bedroom. She was sound asleep.

I knew the police would be on their way to my house since my fiancé and I lived together, but I fought the fear that was trying to paralyze me with the fact that I had not done anything wrong or illegal. I decided to call a taxi to take me to Paula's house. That plan was suddenly changed by a terrifying banging on my front door.

Then I heard a strong voice say, "DEA open up!" Terror gripped my heart, and nervously, I opened the door.

"Are you, Nadine?"

Again, I tried to swallow, but there was nothing to swallow. "Yes," I breathed.

"Do you know someone by the name of Eric Edwards, aka Shawn, aka Mike?" They said all my fiancé's aliases, so I had to answer yes to one.

"Yes, I do," I said.

"We have just arrested him for being a kingpin of a large drug operation that has spanned several states."

I felt frozen, and I could tell there was no expression on my face except a blank stare.

"Ma'am, we do not have a search warrant, but if you don't have anything to hide, you can allow us to search your home without a search warrant," said one of the officers while holding a rifle in his hand and a riot shield over his face.

I told them they could search the house. The house we owned was a four-bedroom, two-story home of about four thousand square feet in a quiet, mid- to upper-class neighborhood. I had never seen illegal activity in that house—neither had I seen drugs nor guns—so I had no qualms allowing them to search the house without a warrant.

I didn't know there would be things found in the house that could be used as key evidence against me in a federal court. They found a bag containing money ($25,000 in cash) and kilos of cocaine. Because the house was solely in my name, they arrested me.

That year I had turned twenty-one years old. I was in my second year of college, pregnant, the mother of a two-year-old, and I was headed to prison. As unreal as my arrest seemed, it wasn't as strange to me as the fact that my aunt had called me a week before and told me she had a dream about me, lying dead in a glass casket located in a glass house. She called me in tears. I gently calmed her fears, and told her I wasn't dead and had no intentions of dying anytime soon.

I, too, had a dream just three days before the police showed up. In the dream, I was being taken to jail. When I told my fiancé of both dreams, he laughed and said if the police ever came to our house, the last person they would take was me since I was just a college girl.

As I sat on my living room couch—feeling the tight, cold, metal handcuff around my wrist, staring across the room at a scared and sleepy two-year-old child—I couldn't help but think of how I wished I had taken heed to those warning signs and many more I had received while involved with Eric.

The officers allowed me to call a classmate to come and pick up my daughter since I had no family living in Virginia. This classmate was a young lady in my pharmacology class who I barely knew. I had her number in my textbook in case of an emergency like missed assignments—not emergencies like this one. She came reluctantly, and the officers patiently waited in the house with me until she arrived, nearly three hours after my call. Had the police decided not to wait, my two-year-old would have been handed over to the custody of the State of Virginia, and who knows what obstacles my family would have had to get her back.

As I sat on the couch for what seemed like eternity, I couldn't help but think of my childhood. What if things had been different? Then I thought of how my daughter's childhood would now be changed forever because of all that was happening in that moment. My life was slipping slowly away. I wanted to cry, but no tears would form. I felt like I was about to pass out, and it was becoming harder and harder for me to breathe.

The feeling reminded me of a time when I was eight years old and away at a summer camp somewhere in upstate New York. While playing a game of capture the flag, which were hidden high in massive oak trees, I was stung by over three hundred bees. I sat for what seemed like hours in the camp nurse's station, covered from head to toes in bees, whose stingers were still stuck in me.

I wanted to cry but couldn't. I could barely breathe. My body had absorbed so much pain that, at that point, I could feel nothing, nor could I speak. I just sat, lightheaded, and stared into the eyes of the nurse. I could see her mouth moving, but could not hear a sound as staff moved frantically trying to scrape the bees off me using their ID cards.

Now, years later, I sat on my living room couch with no expression of feelings while SWAT and DEA officers surrounded me. I couldn't help but think about that experience in upstate New York at summer camp. My eyes dimmed, and I zoned out and traveled down the memory lane of a difficult childhood.

# CHAPTER 2

# A Quest for Love and Acceptance

*You is kind. You is smart. You is important.*

—*The Help*

I HAVE MANY DARK MEMORIES of my childhood; however, I've always tried to focus on the few good times I could remember. Family members told me that I looked a lot like my father—a drummer who traveled with a band that was good enough to play in various countries. He abandoned our family just before I was born, and his absence had a profound negative impact on my life that would follow me for years into my young adulthood.

Not too long after I was born, my mother left Jamaica for America. My older siblings and I remained behind in Jamaica. My sister lived with a family friend, and my brother and I stayed with my aunt— who had six children of her own, along with my grandmother who was battling cancer. It was a full house.

My grandmother was a heavy disciplinarian who was swift with the belt, shoe, or anything she could put her hands on as a tool of correction. I would often receive a painful whipping for misspelled spelling words. As excruciating as that was for me, it did compel me to study hard. Years later I would go on to win the district spelling bee of Brooklyn, New York, and place second runner-up for the state of New York. But the memories of painful beatings left deep emotional scars that would surface throughout my school years as a young teenager.

I have a memory from when I was around four years old that has never left me. I remember going to a beach until sunset with my cousins. I remember the beauty of the beach, the calm waves, and the beautiful sunset as the day was winding down. Unfortunately, that tranquil moment was marred when I received a public whipping in front of a large group of onlookers.

My grandmother was livid that I went to the beach with my cousins and came back at sunset. She thought I was too young to have gone and that it was too late for me to be out. The fact that I was with my older cousins, her grandkids, didn't matter to her. To this day I am still uncertain if that was the real reason for such a severe consequence, but that's what I was told. Unfortunately, that experience has never left my memory bank.

When my mother finally sent for my sister, brother, and me to join her in Brooklyn, New York, I was five years old. The first memory I have of seeing my mother is at John F. Kennedy Airport in New York City. I walked right past her. My older cousin grabbed my hand and pulled me to stand before this beautiful woman as he introduced me to her: "Nadine, this is your mother." I had no feelings. I wanted to feel something but felt no emotion. There would be difficult years ahead when I felt this way often.

There are some good memories I cherish. I didn't have many birthday celebrations, but I do remember celebrating my eighth birthday at Red Robbin's restaurant by Kings Plaza Shopping Center in Brooklyn. I also remember getting the Nike sneakers I wanted for Christmas when I was around ten or eleven years old. These were good memories.

For some reason, I have many blurred and spotty memories of my childhood. While there are other memories that I remember so clearly that I can identify what I was wearing. But in the blurry memories, I see something happening, but the setting and faces are out of focus. These memories always give me a sad, heavy feeling that brings tears to my eyes. It's strange how we carry emotions from childhood experiences into our adulthood. All it takes is a familiar scent or a song or a phrase, and buried memories of long ago are suddenly triggered.

When I was fourteen years old, I found out that from the time of my conception, my life was unwanted. That little piece of information would haunt me for years. When that secret was shared with me, I began to look back on the many occurrences that made me feel like I didn't belong, and it suddenly made sense why I had always thought I wasn't liked much. I would tell myself I belonged, but the words did not match all my childhood experiences. The fact that I was unwanted caused deep feelings that led me to rebel, fight, and give off a lot of attitude.

My childhood was void of hugs and the words "I love you." We didn't have much in my single-parent home in Brooklyn. Our small apartment housed my mother, sister, brother, and me. Us kids shared one bedroom until I was in the tenth grade. My home-life was tumultuous with its many domestic struggles and relational challenges.

During these years I would often think about what a family would look like that was different than mine. I imagined a family where both parents were present in the home and kids came home to family meals at a dinner table with conversations about everyone's day—a family where the words "I love you" were often said to one another. But that was not my reality.

Not only was my home life filled with its fair share of difficulties, but just living in Brooklyn was difficult. As a child and teen in Brooklyn in the eighties, I didn't have the pleasure of just living; I had to learn how to survive. I had to grow up quickly and learn to defend myself at all costs. The streets of New York had a way of toughening your skin whether you wanted it to or not, and Brooklyn was especially brutal, no matter how young you were.

From my elementary-school days, I learned where to walk and where not to walk. I learned when to look and when to look away, pretending I didn't see what I just saw. The streets taught me instincts without me realizing it. The kids in Brooklyn were especially mean to immigrants back in the eighties, especially those like me with a heavy foreign, island accent. I fought a lot to defend myself for being born outside of the Unites States. That's just the way it was.

My mother worked long hours, so whatever I faced at school or had to endure going to and from school, I just had to swallow and deal with it on my own. My stepfather came into the picture and while he was loving toward me and still is, he wasn't much of a talker. There was no going home to tell my parents. My sister and brother were dealing with the same situations—and sometimes worse—because they were older. We all had to suck it up and deal with it in silence.

Children cannot handle this kind of mental and emotional strain. It forced me to emotionally skip over my childhood. Yet, despite these struggles, I loved school and did very well. School was my escape from an emotionally unstable home life. My two favorite subjects were, and still are, history and reading. History helped me discover a bigger world, and I loved obtaining knowledge of true events that helped to shape the course of events. Reading was also a pleasure because I was able to escape to a place the author painted for me. My love of words has helped me become a descriptive communicator.

My fifth-grade teacher, Ms. Lang, would make sure I had plenty of books to read. She was stern but in a nurturing and loving kind of way. I loved her. She was like a mother to me for two years of my life that I will never forget. She always made me feel special and smart even though I had a terrible attitude. I was hurting on the inside each day that I sat in her fifth-grade class. To this day I can identify the perfume she wore, even in a crowded room.

I believe Ms. Lang saw I was an unhappy child who was hurting on the inside. One day I was having a rough day, emotionally. Ms. Lang took notice and told me something I would never forget. She said, "Nadine, you are a very special young lady with a very bright future ahead of you. There are things inside of you that you have yet to discover. When the pain seems too much to bear, escape by writing and reading. The more you read, the better writer you will become." I took that advice to heart.

Writing has helped me get through some dark valleys in my personal life, whether in a prison cell or after a physical abuse. Writing has a way of allowing me to escape to a world that is kind and accepting.

Several years ago I watched a movie called *The Help*. This movie brought me to tears for many reasons. One of the main character was Ms. Aibileen, an African American maid in Mississippi in the 1960s who tended the household of a white family. Ms. Aibileen would dignify the little girl she was hired to care for. This little girl was often neglected by her parents, Ms. Aibileen's employers. But Ms. Aibileen would show the little girl love and care, knowing she lacked this attention from her own parents.

This hired maid did the best she could to fill in the gaps represented in this little girl's life. One of those gaps was to let the little girl know *who she was* as a human being. Ms. Aibileen would get face-to-face with the little girl and tell her, "You is kind. You is smart. You is important."

It was a different setting, different time, and different circumstance, but Ms. Lang was my Ms. Aibileen. While Ms. Lang never said those exact words to me, whenever I was in her presence for those impactful one-on-one talks, she would make me feel like I was kind, I was smart, and I was important. Even if it was way beyond my belief, she often made me feel like I was somebody who was worth something. Though those feelings went as quickly as they came, I was encouraged in the moment.

I was involved in a jump-rope sport called Double Dutch. This sport was very popular in the inner city of New York. It involved two single ropes, two turners and a jumper (or jumpers). To master this sport you had to have tremendous hand and feet coordination. My involvement in this sport, like my schoolwork, was my escape from my home life and it kept me out of trouble as long as it could. Through Double Dutch, I was able to travel to various states and countries doing TV shows, commercials, and competitions. Some of my closest friends to this very day were my Double Dutch teammates. Unfortunately, I didn't have the monetary nor emotional support I needed to continue.

I started becoming numb to the idea of family as my middle-school years came and went. My mom and my sister got along well, and people said they looked alike: pretty. Anytime I was introduced as my mother's daughter, the person's expression said, "No way." I remember once when I was about ten, I was introduced as my mother's daughter, and the lady shook her head and looked utterly repulsed as she said, "My, she looks nothing like you."

I would always remember the disgust on her face. It would be the beginning of a poor self-image. Adults have no idea the weight their words have on young, impressionable minds. My feelings of rejection started with my father's intentional absence, and those feelings started to grow and pick up steam from my middle school years way into my teen and young-adult years. My low self-esteem and my parents' rejection caused a lot of identity issues that impacted many decisions I made as a teenager and even as a young adult.

One thing I was happy about in my younger years, was my relationship with my brother, Gary. I was close with my brother and even dressed like him. We did a lot together, and I wanted to be just like him. He would do anything for me just to see me laugh or break out of a sad mood. Sadly, my brother became mentally ill when I was thirteen years old and was placed in a mental institution. At that time, he was the closest person to me. He brought a piece of security to my turbulent world. Unfortunately, he was hanging with the wrong crowd, smoking marijuana.

We do not know exactly what happened the day of his mental collapse. One evening my coach called me out of my Double-Dutch practice to inform me that he had just received a phone call, and something was wrong with my brother. The callers (my brother's friends) were looking for me. When my coach drove me to the building where my brother was said to be, I found him hiding underneath the staircase of an apartment building in sheer terror. He was screaming that people were trying to get him. Soon afterward he was placed in a mental institution. My brother was only fifteen years old and diagnosed with schizophrenia. He still lives with this diagnosis. What happened to my brother is very difficult to speak about, even to this day.

In my early high-school years, one of my best friends, Tonya, introduced me to a tall and very handsome young man that attended the same high-school as her. He and I started dating. He was a very smart young man who treated me with attention, love, and dignity that I had never experienced before. He made me feel secure, respected and valued. But my home life became too much of a strain, and I started running away, staying at different friends' homes here and there. They didn't know I was running away, since I called it spending the night. But parents began to connect the dots. Eventually, my relationship with this young man would end under the pressure of my tumultuous home life, as well as my street life. Yet our lives would one day cross paths again under very different circumstances—more on that later.

As time went on, I started desiring to have a better relationship with my mother. I started dressing in a more feminine way, so I could look like my mother and sister. But I didn't look right, nor did I feel right. I was very skinny and underdeveloped, physically. But I would begin to wear clothes that would make my twig-frame look more developed. As a teenager, I started working at my mother's club, looking like I was twenty-five. With this new sensual look came much attention. Attention that I could not handle.

The most difficult part was warding off the older men who were constantly making advances toward me, even after I told them my age. The older I dressed and looked, the greater was the burden that come along with my new appearance. Even though I looked older, my look didn't match where I was mentally. I was just a little girl with high heels and lipstick, and I was not capable of handling the pressures and expectations that came along with my new look. Yet, I wanted attention and someone to love me.

Eventually, I would look for the affection I craved in the arms of older men, but at a high cost. Those men gave me tangible gifts—and I accepted them, attempting to fill deep, internal voids—but it was all superficial. Nothing could satisfy the longing within me to feel valued and worthy. Each gift made me feel a sudden rush of value, only to feel empty again. This feeling of emptiness started visiting me more frequently and lasting longer.

I cycled in and out of depression, all while wearing a smile and heels that were too high for me to walk in. This lifestyle would soon spin my life out of control. Trying to find security and love in material things is foolish and proves to be a hole that cannot be filled. The strings attached to the gifts ended up costing me more than I was willing to pay.

CHAPTER 3

# Forbidden Fruits

*Sometimes the fence you are looking at is not there*
*to keep you in but to keep the enemy out.*

THE LIFESTYLE I WAS LIVING was interfering with my academics at school. While I loved school, my grades had dropped drastically from being an *A* student my entire schooling to a low *C* average. My life was now full of gang activity as I continued to look for something or someone to fill the void I constantly felt inside.

My sister was my role model, and I wanted to act like her, look like her, and get the attention she commanded everywhere she went. I tried in many ways to imitate her, and while she had her own struggles, her issues rarely surfaced, to me.

As I mentioned I looked nothing like my sister or my mother. I looked a lot like my father, who had a darker complexion. I had no issue with this until people started pointing out that fact each time I was introduced as one of my mother's children. The stares I would get made me feel more and more, that something was wrong with me.

My sister and I were night and day. She was girly, and I was a tomboy. She didn't fight unless she absolutely had to. I, on the other hand, had no qualms with throwing a mean punch or two in the blink of an eye. I carried handguns, knives, and even razors in my mouth. I remember almost killing one of my closest friends while I was playing around with a revolver that was loaned to me at the time. I pointed the gun at point-blank range next to her head and jokingly asked her if I could pull the trigger. Not knowing exactly how revolvers worked, I pulled the trigger, and by the grace of God, she ducked her head at the same time. We all ran for cover, and our ears rang for hours from the blast of the gun. The bullet had missed her head by milliseconds. That impulsive action could have led to her death and to me being put away in prison, possibly for the rest of my life. That wasn't the only time God spared me in such a way.

Not too long after that incident, an old gang-related beef was stirred up in Franklyn Avenue train station while I was on my way home from school. This particular train station was known for turf wars, gang-related fights, and even deaths. The incident escalated inside the train station until a mob of people led us outside to have a one-on-one and fight it out. Some of this massive crowd were on the side of the girl I had an issue with, and some were on my side, while others were neutral. Make no mistake about it, everyone was there to be entertained—the bloodier, the more entertaining it would be for the onlookers.

Just before this girl and I began to fight, I slipped a brass knuckle onto my right hand. I held her head with my left hand and pounded the brass knuckle into her head with my right. It was bloody to say the least. When police arrived, they asked me for the weapon I used. While they were approaching me to search me, a friend of mine slipped behind me and pulled the brass knuckle off my hand. This task was very difficult because my hand was stuck in a fist position, making it hard for her to slip the brass knuckles from my fingers.

The officers found nothing on me and let me go. For months the girl's aunt, who was a high-ranked correction officer at Riker's Island Prison in New York, tried to get charges drawn against me but to no avail. I was told she had a squad of prisoners waiting for the day I would come to that prison. But it was not my time to enter prison just yet.

That was my world, but it was very different from my sister's world. As time went on, I started doing my best to look more like a girl and started trying my best to act like one. However, I still had a bad attitude and fought a lot. This was the period I mentioned when I started to look more and more feminine and when I was working in my mother's club. She would warn me not to entertain conversations with older men, just to keep it business related. No explanations of why were given, just "stay away." But I didn't follow her advice for too long.

I would go to school in the day and work at the club in the evenings and on weekends, where I met men who were much older than me. Eventually, I ventured into a life of money, shopping sprees, and parties. It cost me my body, and on a few occasions, it almost cost me my life.

I think I was about sixteen years old when I saw Eric for the first time. He was twenty-seven and very attractive and popular with young and old alike. He didn't dress that well, but he sure was confident...and he was way out of my league. At the time I was just starting to dress in a more feminine way, but for the most part, I was still a tomboy.

One day while working at the club and looking very sensual, I heard that Eric was inquiring about me. I was shocked that such a powerful man was interested in little ole me. He hung out with famous rappers and had older, mature women at his beck and call. He could have any female he wanted. *Why me?* I wondered.

We were formally introduced, exchanged phone numbers, and started having daily conversations. Eric started taking me out on expensive dates until the relationship escalated and became more serious. We went on shopping sprees and ate in high-end restaurants in various states. We hung out with rappers and celebrities in the music industry. It was unreal.

One day while visiting him in Virginia, I was in his condo alone when I heard a knock on the door. When I opened the door, I found it was the police, and I asked them how could I help them. They told me they had Eric in police custody, and he had told them I was in the house with bags of drugs and that the drugs were all mine. My response was a skeptical, "Excuse me?"

They asked if they could search the house, and I told them sure. After searching for about an hour, they found nothing. After the search a female officer walked with me from the living room to one of the bedrooms to question me. While we were in the bedroom, one of the officers yelled aloud, "Well, well, what have we here? Drugs?"

When we got to the room where the officers were, I saw an enormous black garbage bag filled with a white, powdery substance. This was absolutely bogus since they had been searching a two-bedroom condo for over an hour and found nothing but suddenly a large, human sized trash bag just mysteriously appears in one of the bed-rooms—not to mention I had been in that room several times that day, and there had been no such bag.

"One of you put that there because that wasn't there when you searched not too long ago," I said. I told them they were trying to frame me, and after a while they realized they couldn't fool me. After that they drove me to the police station for questioning, where they realized I was clueless about what was going on.

They released me at about half past eleven o'clock at night with no money and no idea where I was. When I asked if someone could take me back to the condo, they all said in unison, "No!"

"Can you at least point me in the direction of the apartment so I can start walking?"

One officer responded, "that way" while pointing in two different di-rections at the same time. The entire room of officers started laughing. I walked out of that station and started walking down a highway with barely any streetlights in the darkness of the Virginia night. About forty-five minutes after I started walking, I heard someone yelling to me from a nearby gas station. I looked ahead and kept on walking.

The person eventually drove up and offered to give me a ride. I saw the cross hanging from his rearview mirror and a Bible on his dashboard and figured maybe it would be safe. I told him that I was visiting from New York; however, the person that I was visiting was now in police custody. Since I didn't know the condo's address, he asked if I could remember what was in the area of the condo complex where I was staying. I was able to recall some things, and as we drove around looking for the complex, he told me about his family. We talked about his kids who were my age and older, and he told me he was a deacon at his church.

I thought how lucky I was for this good, church man to have picked me up in the middle of nowhere, and now here he was helping me get out of an unfortunate situation. I was grateful. After a little over an hour of driving, I was relieved to finally arrive at the condo. He told me he would take me to the local Greyhound bus station, so I was to grab my belongings from the condo and hurry along since the police had told me they were giving me twelve hours to get out of their state.

As I was climbing out of the truck, this *hospitable* deacon grabbed my hand and asked me what was I going to give him in return for him helping me. I told him I had no money, but I was very grateful. He told me what I could give him didn't require money. I could feel my heart burning.

I remembered being thirteen years old and alone with my cousin's boyfriend, in his car, as he had promised my cousin he would take me home from her house because she was running late for work. He was much older than I was and much stronger, and there was no one to stop the abuse. That would be the first of three separate experiences of rape that I would experience.

Fast forward several years later, and the same feeling of terror came rushing back as the man who I thought was helping me held onto my arm with a forceful grip. Through my tears, I reminded him of his kids and his church that he told me about. He said that had nothing to do with what was owed to him. I pleaded with him, saying I just wanted to get to the bus station before the police arrived. I think the mention of police startled him. He yelled and told me to hurry up and get my stuff before he changed his mind about taking me to the bus station. That drive to the bus station was scary and quiet.

Looking back, I now realize how dangerous it was for me to get back in the van with that perverted stranger. I guess I was so scared and desperate to get out of the state that I didn't think through that decision. He did not pay for my ticket back to New York like he said he would, but I was just happy to be at the bus station and out of his vehicle, safely. I called one of my closest friends, and she and her older brothers drove from New York to Virginia and picked me up from the bus station. I was sixteen years old.

Eric was deported out of the United States, but it would not be the last time our paths would cross.

That incident shook me up a bit, but after a few months, I went back to living the life I had become accustomed to: working in my mother's club and hanging out with all the wrong people, going to all the wrong places. But now I had developed feelings of fear and paranoia. Fear attacks your peace and your ability to enjoy life. So, I looked to men for a sense of protection and security. But these men also had fears of their own; they just hid their feelings behind masks of material possessions and thug-like attitudes.

I would often think back to the deacon; even he wore a mask. He hid behind the Bible so he could pretend to be someone he wasn't. God's Word was on his dashboard, but that was as close as it got to him. God's Word had certainly never entered his heart to change his soul. He lived one way outwardly in front of people, even his family, while he was someone different on the inside.

The men I was getting involved with found their sense of security in the amount of things they possessed, but the very things they thought they possessed actually possessed them because whatever controls you is actually your master. Whether money, men, women, material possessions, drugs, alcohol, the limelight, or other things, when people are driven by what they possess or what they are trying to possess, they become slaves to that thing.

When my mother warned me of the forbidden fruit, she was putting an invisible fence around me to protect me, but I saw it as a cage that I needed to escape. Had she explained her reasons to me, I might have listened. I wanted love and security, but I was looking for it in the wrong places. The people I was trying to get it from could not provide it to me because they were also looking for the same things I was. It was the blind leading the blind and getting nowhere.

I remember the day I looked at my life in absolute disgust of what it had become. In my quest to find love and acceptance, I had lost the Nadine who once had hopes and dreams. I started becoming someone I did not recognize.

# CHAPTER 4

# But God Had a Purpose

*I firmly believe that in every situation, no matter*
*how difficult, God extends grace greater than the*
*hardship, and strength and peace of mind that can lead*
*us to a place higher than where we were before.*

*—Andy Griffith*

AT THE START OF MY twelfth grade year of High School I found out I was pregnant—a one night decision with lasting consequences. The father was an older gentleman who I had no intention of being with long term. One night in a club, led to one mistake that would push my life in an entirely unplanned direction. My life had spun out of control with men, partying, abuse, and now an unwanted pregnancy with no one to turn to. Slowly, I started to forget about the Nadine of old who once hoped for a better tomorrow. My fifth grade teacher's words had long faded into oblivion with no plans of returning. That future was just a fairy tale that would never be.

Having a baby at eighteen wasn't how I thought my life would end up. I wanted to go to college, graduate, and have a wonderful career as a psychologist. Now, here I was pregnant for someone who was twelve years older than me, of whom I had no desire to be with long term.

I wasn't surprised when my mother made it very clear I could not live in her house and give birth to a child. I decided to have an abortion. I made the appointment with the abortion clinic, but each time I went, there was some confusion or mistake with the appointment date.

The longer I took to have the abortion, the more this baby was growing and moving inside of me. I remember driving to the abortion clinic in a new car, and all of a sudden, the front right tire came off and rolled into the street! But I was determined not to have this baby. At six months pregnant, the clinic could no longer do the abortion because the pregnancy was too far along, so they made an appointment for me to get the procedure done at a local hospital in Brooklyn.

I went to the hospital, and the doctor took a sonogram and saw two cysts growing on my fallopian tubes. He explained that if I had the abortion, there was an 80 percent chance that I would not be able to have children in the future.

"It's ok," I said. "I don't want kids anyway."

The doctor looked puzzled and concerned. Throughout the exam he kept staring at me sadly.

*What is up with this doctor?* I thought. He asked if it would be ok if he spoke with my parents, which actually broke hospital protocol. I told him sure, but he would be wasting his time since my parent agreed with my decision 100 percent. He called my mother and explained my medical condition, and she asked him if she could speak with me.

To my surprise my mother was crying on the other end of the phone, explaining that she did not want me to grow up and hate her for allowing me to go through with the abortion, especially since there was a high probability I would not be able to have kids in the future. She said if I kept the baby, she would stay with the baby while I finished school (although she really couldn't because of her club business). I decided not to get an abortion.

I took night classes the rest of my senior year because my morning sickness was so severe. I graduated a couple months early during the spring while I was still pregnant. A couple months after I graduated, I had a beautiful little girl. I didn't have a name picked out for her so on the spot, in the hospital room, my best friend and I named her, Tenae. We just combined the beginning of both of our names to quickly provide to the seemingly annoyed lady that was needing to complete the birth certificate form. After Tenae was born, I couldn't imagine my life without her; however, I was not ready to be a mother, and I was irresponsible in many ways.

It was very hard to go to college full time, be a mother, and to live the diva life I chose. Parties, guys, and sleeping out on school nights were a normal routine for me. I was what one would call an unfit teen mother. My body was mature enough to have a child, but the rest of me wasn't.

One day when I was at home, there was a knock on my door. It was a close friend from my childhood whom I had not seen in years. In fact, it was one of Eric's family members. I was shocked to see her at my front door. She told me she had a surprise to show me, and I saw a shadowy figure in the dark. It was Eric.

*I thought he was deported. How is it that he is standing at my front door?* I felt numb. I had pushed him to the back of my mind and stifled the feelings I had for him. Now, as I stood staring at him, those old feelings started to resurface. Not too long after that evening, Eric and I started seeing each other again. My mother said that if I continued seeing Eric, I would have to get out of her house. After several weeks of arguments and a physical altercation with my mother, I moved out of her house. I was nineteen years old, and Eric was thirty-one.

At that time Eric didn't have any money, and neither did I. I really don't know how we made it. I had left behind my mother's brand new clean three-story house in Brooklyn that we had been living in since my tenth grade year of High School. But due to a physical altercation between my mother and I, I moved out of her house with my toddler daughter. We ended up living in an abandoned, critter-infested brownstone among crack addicts. It was a sad, depressing situation, but I was angry and too hurt to try and make amends with my mother. Yet, in trying to punish my mother, I put my daughter through a lot. To this day she will scream the roof down if she sees a roach.

After some time Eric told me he had purchased a laundromat and a car wash in Virginia, and both businesses seemed to be doing very well. Eric started rolling in money with his new businesses, and I started going to college again. We finally moved out of the abandoned brownstone building and settled in a nice town house in Virginia.

After a while we started buying nice things, including a luxury SUV for which we paid $50,000 in cash. We went to a lot of music-industry events and parties and were often around well-known R&B artists and rappers. We had so much money we didn't know what to do with it—although we did everything but save or spend wisely.

I tried to get Eric to open a bank account, but he wouldn't hear of it. All his money was kept in a big safe in the house that not even I had the combination to. But the more money we had, the more paranoid he became. This new lifestyle brought nothing but enemies, violence, fear, and kidnappings into our lives. No one could be trusted.

I am reminded of two incidents that happened about three months apart during this time of financial overabundance. We had decided to build a house, and while our new house was being worked on, we stayed with Eric's cousin until our house was move-in ready. She lived a very flashy and flamboyant lifestyle, and she was also a no-nonsense kind of woman who could easily back up any threat she made.

Her and Eric were business partners and had a close relationship. One day Eric and her got into a violent argument about money. Eric decided he would leave immediately and take his enormous safe with him. The safe was very heavy, so Eric needed someone who had a truck to help him move it. He called some friends that he had previously done jail time with. He didn't want to call family members because he didn't want his cousin to know he was leaving.

The guys came and loaded the safe. Our car was at the dealership getting some custom work done, so Eric drove in one car with the safe and a couple of the guys, and I rode in another car. I was in the back seat of the car, with my toddler on my lap, and two guys whom I had never met before were in the front.

About ten o'clock that night, both cars pulled up at a house—Eric's car in front of mine—where they were to drop off the safe, Eric, and my daughter and me. When we pulled into the wide-open driveway, Eric got out of the car to explain to the people inside that he would be bringing the safe in the house and leaving it there until the work on our house was completed. He trusted the people in the house— whom I had never heard of.

Suddenly, the car that still had the safe in it reversed around us and peeled out of the driveway. The guys in the car I was in looked at each other, and then the driver backed out, speeding down the road as well. I was sitting in the back seat trying to process what was happening. I'm thinking, *"I don't remember seeing Eric get back into that car…Isn't he still in the house?"*

Before I knew it, we were on the Chesapeake Bay Bridge silently driving at an intense speed. Suddenly, the guy sitting in the passenger seat turned around, pointed a gun directly in my toddler's face and yelled, "Why you ain't just get out the car? Now you gonna die like this? The plan was for you to get out the car and go into the house with Eric-but ok, you're choice!"

No words would form in my mind to respond to this crazy, demented looking fool. He turned around and started mumbling under his breath. I was trying to think as fast as I could of how in the world am I going to get my daughter out of this car, alive. I kept looking back out the back window, hoping to see flashing lights of a police car, but all I could see were headlights of cars driving behind us on the bridge. Interrupting my frantic thoughts, the gunman turned around again and started yelling that he was going to blow my daughter's head off, and my daughter started screaming at the top of her lungs.

"Listen here, I'm going to give you five seconds to jump out of this car or both of y'all getting bullets to your heads." And you could tell by looking at his cold eyes that he meant every word. Basically, my choice was to die by a gunshot or by jumping out of a speeding car onto a bridge with oncoming traffic. He started counting and held the gun at my daughter's head. I was more terrified for my daughter's life than I was for mine.

I cried and begged if they could just slow down the car so I could jump out, but he kept counting down from five. The car was going so fast that each time I opened the car door, the wind against the door would shut it, not giving me an opportunity to jump out. "Two," he counted. I closed my eyes so tight it hurt, and then I uttered my first real attempt at prayer: "God, if you are real, save us."

When I went to jump, the back door was wide open as if the car was in a parked position with its door open. I then leaped onto the Chesapeake Bay Bridge and waited for the feeling of a car colliding right into my baby and me. After a long pause, I opened my eyes, and—to my amazement—I had landed in a seated position with my daughter on my lap facing the oncoming traffic. There was not one car driving on that bridge on the side where I was. The heel on my right shoe was broken, and that was the extent of any physical damage my daughter and I sustained. I limped off that bridge with my baby in hand and a broken heel, carelessly thanking God for saving us but not thinking of Him again.

About three months after the robbery, Eric and his cousin buried the hatchet, and we were at her house for a family social. This was the same house where the men who robbed Eric had picked up the safe. Word was on the street that Eric was offering a lot of money to anyone who could direct him to the guys who robbed him (although the so-called friends were never caught).

About two o'clock in the morning, Eric and his cousin got into a big altercation about money. It was so intense that a couple others who were in the house had to get in between them. We were hours away from our house, so we left and went to Eric's brother's house—about twenty minutes away from where we were.

While at Eric brother's house, his sister-in-law turned on the TV while she prepared her kids for school. I could hear the 6:00 a.m. news playing as Eric, my daughter, and I were in the guest bedroom down the hall. I clearly heard the news reporter say, "breaking news from…" and she stated an address that sounded very familiar to me. I jumped out of the bed and ran toward the living room to watch the broadcast. The news story was about Eric's cousin's house—the one we had just left a few hours before. Apparently, the guys who robbed us three months earlier heard that Eric was looking for them, and they wanted to act first. Everyone in the house was killed by gunshot wounds, including a sweet thirteen-year-old boy. I was in absolute shock. I couldn't believe I was watching a house with caution signs taped all around it and I was just sitting in there hours before with my toddler. *"That could have been me and my daughter,"* I thought. The gunmen arrived less than two hours after we left.

# CHAPTER 5

# Something Is after My Life

ERIC AND I HAD EVERYTHING except peace and joy. We forfeited peace for temporary material possessions. No matter how much we had, there was always an inner emptiness that neither could satisfy for the other. There were many abusive fights, and I lived in fear for my life and my daughter's life. Eric lived in fear of who would try to kill him for what he possessed. He had a lot, but couldn't enjoy it because of fear.

Eric lived in a mental world where no one could be trusted—not the grocery clerk, not the professors at my college, not even the kindergarten teacher at my daughter's school. No one was to be trusted because everyone was out to get him. He lived in a constant state of looking over his shoulder, even suspicious of his own family. We would take a different route home almost every day. Fear loomed all around us and paranoia began to overtake Eric's mind.

Eric's life was void of purpose and hope, and so was mine. With all the material possession we had, that time of my life was the emptiest point I have ever experienced.

I've come to realize that the enemy is not just out for you physically, but he is after what's inside you. He's after your hopes, your dreams, your aspirations, and your future. To make it simple, he's after your purpose. That's why he works against us from childhood. He will cause us to suffer rejection, loneliness, and words of defeat spoken over us. He'll have us experience atrocities of all kinds—like forms of abuse—to work against our self-esteem and identity. He lures us into unhealthy relationships so that we would trade the life God intends for us to experience a counterfeit one.

Many things have happened in my life to cause me to want to give up on life—things meant to deceive me into thinking my life is not worth living. But deep down—buried under the pain, the hurt, and the abuse—was a girl who believed…even if it was just a little belief. I never vocalized such a crazy thought, but deep within me somewhere, I had a tiny belief that there was more for my life than the things I had experienced. The problem was, I had no clue how to find that better life. Years later I would come to realize that the enemy was more concerned with stopping me than I was concerned with discovering a better life.

There are two unrelated incidents that took place in my life that made me realize something or someone was after me. One of these two incidents took place when I was in elementary school, and the other happened when I was a young adult. There have been many other instances—some of which I choose not to share in this book because of its graphic nature—however, as I look back on these two incidents, they lead me to believe that the hand of God was there to protect me from a very early age and to deliver me from the enemy's plan to end my life.

One incident took place when I was just seven years old. I was allowed to walk to school by myself at this young age, and my school was about three New York City blocks from my house, with only one major crossing section where there was always a school-crossing guard.

One spring morning I was walking to school by myself, as I did every school morning (although there were a lot of other kids walking to school too because there were two schools in our neighborhood: an elementary school and a junior-high school).

I approached the crossing light where the crossing guard was directing traffic, and waited patiently for her to give me the signal to cross. As I was waiting, I noticed the two Doberman pinscher dogs in the yard of the corner house just catty-corner from where I was standing. I had seen the dogs ever since we moved into that

Brooklyn neighborhood, but that morning there was something different about one of the dogs. It kept staring directly at me.

Kids were all around, but the dog had his eyes locked only on me. I would move around just a little, and sure enough, the dog would turn his head and follow my every move. As I watched the dog, I also watched the crossing guard waiting for her to give the signal for me to cross. I noticed the dog started running toward the fence of the yard and attempting to jump over it over and over.

Now, these dogs were huge. They both stood much taller than my seven-year-old, slender frame. I looked around and noticed no one was watching what was happening. Finally, the dog's attempts paid off. He jumped over the fence, dashed past every child in his proximity, and hurtled toward me.

The crossing guard, totally unaware of what was happening behind her, motioned for me to cross, but I was frozen with fear. Then something happened I would never forget. The crossing guard held her stop sign in the direction of oncoming cars, as she stood in the middle of the street and motioned again to me to cross the street. Suddenly, a car sped through the red light at the intersection, past the crossing guard, and had a head-on collision with the dog. The dog flew up in the air and landed on its head.

I could not believe what had just happened. Finally, my brain communicated with my legs, and I silently crossed the street amid the chaos around me—although I wanted to run and keep on running, forever. I could hear the cry of that dog as I walked down the block and turned into the school's entry doors.

Years later I realized that had I crossed when the crossing guard motioned for me to cross, had I not been paralyzed in terror, I would have walked right into the speeding car. It would have been my body flying into the air and landing lifeless on that Brooklyn intersection. But God had a plan for my life even then.

The second incident took place in 1995, just before my life came to a screeching halt because of my incarceration. Eric and I were still living very comfortably. I was young and had everything I wanted (materialistically speaking): diamonds, a big house, a nice SUV, and shopping sprees every weekend. But the more money Eric obtained, the more insecure he became.

His jealousy (which always led to physical rage) was out of control, and I was becoming more and more afraid of him as the emotional and physical abuse increased. I wanted to leave and tried to several times, but that proved to be very dangerous for both me and my daughter.

I remember once, after I was terribly abused by Eric, due to one of his fits of jealous rage, Eric was asleep in the upstairs bedroom. I stayed awake until I knew he was in a deep sleep, and then I quietly got up and went to my daughter's room where I called a cab. I asked specifically for the cab driver to park at the end of the road and told the service that I would meet the cab there at the time of arrival. I explained that I was trying to get my daughter and myself to safety, so it was important that he did as I said and not pull up in front of the house.

The cab driver told me to come out in fifteen minutes. At around four o'clock in the morning, I sat quietly in the dark with a garbage bag filled with some clothes for my daughter and myself. She was fast asleep on the living room couch as I paced slowly back and forth looking out the front window for the cab driver. My heart was pounding at the thought that we were finally about to be free.

I was afraid, but I knew I needed to get us out of the dangerous situation we were living in. The time finally came, and I slowly got up from the couch, went outside, and placed the bag of clothes in the taxi cab. I went back into the house to pick up my sleeping daughter and tiptoed slowly in the dark toward the door. As I slowly quietly turned the doorknob, I heard a firm voice say, "Now, you can just turn around and put Tenae in her bed and tell that cab driver to get lost if he doesn't want any problems."

I did exactly what Eric said with tears running down my face. Unknown to me, Eric had a hidden monitor in my daughter's bedroom that had picked up my call to the taxi service. I felt like I was stuck with no way out. I always felt that the next attempt I made to leave Eric would be my last because he would kill me. He made this very clear, and I believed him. It seemed, though, that he would have to get in line with his death wish because whatever it was that was after my life since birth was determined to end my life at all cost.

But that was not the incident in 1995 that demonstrated God's protection on my life. In summer of 1995, Eric, Tenae, and I were driving to New York to visit my family. Eric believed that if I ever went to New York by myself, I would not return, and he was right.

Eric was tired, so I drove. He quickly fell asleep in the passenger seat and Tenae, who was still a toddler, was sleeping on the back seat. None of us had on our seatbelts. It was a clear, beautiful summer afternoon. After driving for about 2 hours and we were passing through Washington, DC, on I-395. I was driving doing a speed of about ninety miles per hour (hey, don't judge me.) The windows were down, the wind was blowing, Sade's CD was playing, and I was cruising.

At this particular stretch of I-395, there were about five lanes going north, and I felt like someone was staring at me from the car to my left. I paid no attention and sped up. A little later I had the same feeling, so I sped up just like before. When it happened a third time, I was extremely annoyed, so I looked to my left and saw an older white man in a burgundy Lincoln Town Car. He smiled at me, and I turned my head and sped up once again. But as I drove I realized something that made the hair on my arms and on the back of my neck stand to attention. An eerie feeling came over me as I quickly pulled the fact from the archives of my mind that the man who was driving in the lane next to me was the same man who had tried to kidnap me years ago when I was fourteen. I could not believe it!

I looked in his direction again and saw something I do not speak about often because it's unexplainable. When I looked at the man's face again, it looked as if he had no eyes in his eye sockets—only dark holes. His face began to look distorted, and I was scared out of my mind.

Before I could yell for Eric, the man rammed his car into mine. I was in the second lane from the right lane of the five-lane highway, and I was doing a bit above ninety miles per hour when my car spun out of control going across every lane on the I-395. I knew it would be a matter of seconds before several cars hit us dead on. Even though everything seemed to be moving in slow motion, I could not get the car under control, so I gave up trying.

Eric woke up and calmly told me to remove my foot from the brake pedal. He grabbed the steering wheel with one hand and moved it in the direction the car was going until we slowed down to a stop on the grass beside the highway. People got out of their cars and ran toward us to see if we were ok. There was a lady who walked over to us and stated that she saw the driver of the other car intentionally rammed his car into the direction of my car, and said she would stay until the police arrived to give her eyewitness account of what happened. But Eric left before the police could get there. We drove off without a scratch on our vehicle!

I was in shock—not because we almost died but because the same man who had just tried to kill us with his burgundy Lincoln Town Car looked exactly like the man who had tried to kidnap me when I was a teenager. I believe that man was a device used of the enemy to once again try and end my life.

I often wondered about the slow-motion aspect of the accident. I believe the Lord was allowing me to see how precious life is and to also show me I was not in control of my own life, for if it had not been for Him in these situations and many more, I would not be alive to tell about it.

I can't explain why God continued to spare my life even when I did not acknowledge Him. All I can say is that God's love for us goes far beyond our lack of love for Him. God was very patient with me, far more than I deserved. Unfortunately, even though I kept seeing God's caution signs, I ignored them.

One day I again built up enough courage to leave with Tenae while Eric was out. I ended up at an acquaintance's house and explained my situation to her. She said my daughter and I could stay the night since the next Greyhound bus for New York was leaving at six thirty the next morning.

Late that night, while Tenae and I were asleep, Eric showed up at the house. I thought I was having a nightmare. He would later tell me that I had no friends, and that he was all I had. My acquaintance had contacted Eric and told him I was at her house, and if he would Western Union her $800 to pay her rent, she would give him the address, which he did.

She had no idea that she nearly caused my death that night for one month's rent. By this time I was begging for death to somehow catch up to me because the turmoil I was living in was far too great. Then I would wonder about who would take care of Tenae, and I felt stuck and hopeless.

One Saturday afternoon while driving to the mall, I felt as though a car was following me, but I shook off the feeling. While I was walking around the mall, it seemed as though two men were entering every store as I was leaving. It seemed strange because these were clearly stores marketed toward the urban female, and these men were white with a middle-class, suburban look. They wore dark sunglasses with jeans, polo shirts neatly tucked into their jeans, and sneakers.

I shook off the feeling, but I was actually under surveillance for months. Everywhere I went, every phone call I made, every gymnastics class my daughter attended, the detectives were there capturing everything with pictures and video recordings. My lawyer would try to use these photos and recordings in my defense to prove I had nothing to do with Eric's illegal affairs, but to no avail.

That dreadful day I was sitting in my living room, handcuffed, one of the surveillance officers said, "You know we saved you and your daughter's life." He later explained that not only was Eric getting high on drugs and losing his mental grasp, but also, while they had us under heavy surveillance, the officers came across a hit that was placed on us—one that was paid for by a rival drug lord who wanted territory that Eric controlled. He told me the hit was planned for the week of my arrest.

God loves us so much that He will do whatever it takes to save us from ourselves. Often, it's not the outside factors that pose the greatest threat to us, but it's what is within us. Our desires can be severely destructive, and our increasing appetite for the things that are unhealthy can be detrimental to the life God desires for us. The things I thought I wanted were actually hijacking the life God intended for me to have.

CHAPTER 6

# Nightmare but Not a Dream

"Take off all your clothes, squat, bend over, cough!" said the deputy as she looked at me with cold green eyes. "Spread your butt cheeks! Turn around! Open your mouth! Stick out your tongue!" she yelled.

The way she looked at me, you would think I was a criminal or something. *This must be a bad dream*, I thought over and over to myself. I was in jail and was in complete disbelief. Each time I went to sleep, I hoped I would awaken from this nightmare. I just couldn't believe I was in jail because there were drugs found in a house that was in my name.

*"Hopefully, they will realize that I've never sold drugs or taken drugs and, with great regret, they will release me from this godforsaken place."* I thought to myself.

A few weeks after being granted bail, my bail had been revoked. Federal agents had arrested me while at work in Manhattan, in front of my boss and co-workers. It was a humiliating and scary moment for me. One minute I am at work in a prestigious design firm in Manhattan, and the next minute I'm being hauled off into a black, unmarked car with handcuffs on. The prosecutor was able to convince the judge that my bail should be revoked because I was a flight risk, and that I would not show up for trial in Virginia. I was placed in the Manhattan Detention Complex, a municipal jail in lower Manhattan. While in the jail, I was under such severe stress that after a few weeks of being there, I woke up covered in blood from the waste down. The jail guards put me in a wheelchair and brought me to the nurse station to be examined but there were no signs on my body to indicate where the blood was coming from. I told them that I felt some cramping in my stomach area. The ambulance came and took me to the nearby hospital, in handcuffs, where I found out that I had a miscarriage. I was somewhat relieved. Here I was pregnant, in jail, and the father of the child was also in jail. And neither of us knew how long we would be there. So, a miscarriage at four months pregnant was a blessing in disguise, I thought. I stayed in the hospital for one night, handcuffed to a bed and was brought back to the jail the following afternoon. About a week later, the marshals showed up unannounced and moved me and several other inmates into an unmarked van.

The two marshals drove in silence for what seemed like hours. We weren't allowed to wear a watch, so I had no clue how long we drove. They drove us to a remote area that looked like a huge airplane strip. I saw no buildings, just a big, open space and several watchtowers with one military-looking officer with binoculars at each tower.

When I got out of the van, I was shocked by what I saw: prisoners as far as the eyes could see. Some were dressed in orange jumpsuits, identical to the one I wore, while others wore khaki shirts and matching khaki pants. There were men and women lined up by sections. These prisoners were young and old and of different races, nationalities, and ethnic groups. Marshals dressed in black SWAT-like uniforms and wearing aviator sunglasses were standing around the perimeter of the airport strip. Each held a machine gun.

There were enormous planes parked between various sections of the massive group of people. These planes were to take us to whatever prison or state jails we were being sent to. I later learned that some of the prisoners were being transported to serve time in a long-term prison facility, not a holding county jail like the one where I had been. Some prisoners were going to court in another state to face new charges or to be tried for existing charges.

Transporting prisoners was a big deal for security reasons. Prisoner-transportation vehicles could be ambushed if a prisoner somehow communicated that he or she was being moved at a certain time, to a certain location. Therefore, the federal marshals made sure everything was done in a covert way and under heavy security. Each prisoner entered a designated plane to take him or her to a predetermined location.

We were all shackled around our ankles and around our wrist, which was attached to a chain around our waist. I was mute with shock and fear. As they marched us onto these massive planes, the men sat toward the front, and they marched us women, single file, to seats in the back of the plane. I quickly noticed how black men outnumbered every other demographic present.

None of us knew where we were headed. I ended up going to a large holding facility, which I later found out was in Oklahoma City. That was my first time in Oklahoma. During my intake, I was processed by a woman who looked very manly. She wore no makeup, and she had a male physique. She was visibly aggressive in her speech and movements. She asked me for my ID number and became visibly annoyed because I did not have this number memorized and instead gave her my full name.

I told her I had only been in the system a couple months, and she replied by grunting and giving me a long, cold stare. She then said to me, in a very intimidating way, that as long as I was incarcerated I would no longer be referred to by name, so I had better know my federal number by memory because I was just another prisoner with a number in the system. I was then told to take everything off and follow her directions as she searched every part of my body from head to toe. It was dehumanizing.

I stayed in that facility for about one month. I was able to speak with the lawyer who told me he had been in touch with my family. He told me I was in a transfer facility, where prisoners make stops on their way to different jails and prisons for various reasons. He said not even he knew the exact location of the facility. His last words to me were "stay out of trouble."

While at this facility, I spoke to no one outside my cell. I stayed in my room and only came out to eat and take a shower. I had one roommate name Sarah. She was from Mexico. She told me she had three small children that she needed to get home to because she told them she would be right back, and that was three years ago. I was in absolute shock as I considered my own situation. That was the extent of our communication for the time we were cellmates in that facility.

Sarah prayed and sang songs the entire time I was there, and it annoyed the heck out of me. All day, every day, I heard, *Demos gracias Al Senor Demos gracias, Demos gracias Al Senor. Por las mananas las aves cantan las alabanzas a Cristo Salvador. Y tú amigo, ¿porque no cantas las alabanzas de Cristo el Salvador?* To this day, I know that entire song, and I don't even speak Spanish. The English translation says, *Let us give thanks to the Lord, let us give thanks for his love. In the morning the birds sing the praises of Christ, the Savior. And you, friend, why don't you sing praises to Christ, the Savior?* Now that I know the English translation, I understand why Sarah sang that song all day, every day. Many people in prison use different things to cope with the prison environment and all that it forces on you. Sarah sang songs of praise to God to help get her through and to give her hope. Prison can strangle out of you, every ounce of hope that you try to cling to.

Other prisoners choose more self-destructive habits—always easier to find in prison than healthy habits. When I finally left that facility, I went through the same process I had experienced to get there. Marshals arrived at my cell unannounced early one morning, and I was escorted to a van, taken to an open airport space, and marched single file to the back of a massive plane. Only difference was that this time I wore a khaki shirt and matching khaki pants.

This plane landed in Virginia. About twelve of us were escorted to a van where federal marshals awaited us. As I sat at a window seat staring out a tinted window, I couldn't help but think about my two-year-old daughter. I hadn't spoken to my family since I had called to say my bail had been revoked, and I had been arrested for the second time. That was the extent of that phone call with my mother. My stepfather came on the phone to finish the rest of the conversation concerning my whereabouts. I told him to tell my daughter I loved her, and I would be home soon. As much as I wanted to believe that, deep down I knew I was lying. What gave me some consolation is knowing that my daughter was living with her grandparents and they would care for her and keep her safe while I was in prison.

As I sat in the marshal's transportation van, I wondered if my daughter was aware that I had been gone for several months. I wondered if she was sad and if she was asking for me. I kept wondering what I had done to deserve this life. *I should have just stayed away from guys with expensive cars and motorcycles*, I thought. *I didn't know it would cost me this much.*

After arriving at the jail, every part of me was strip-searched again. Then I was led into a temporary holding cell. The following day the FBI came to pick me up to go through rounds of interrogation. These federal agents were not as nice as the DEA officers who waited in my living room for someone to pick up my daughter. After I told them repeatedly that I did not know anything about Eric's drug business, they were enraged and threatened that I would spend at least twenty-five years in prison.

*That is impossible,* I thought to myself. *What have I done? They're just trying to scare me.* Time would prove that I was wrong. On the contrary, the district attorney would seek a sentence to put me away for twenty-five years, just as the officers said. When they returned me to the jail cell, my stomach felt knotted with tension. What I was facing was real, and there didn't seem to be anything I could do about it.

At the time I arrived at the county jail, the facility was overcrowded, so I was given a thin mattress and a piece of real estate on the cement floor, where I would sleep for the first three days. After that my assigned cell was a six-foot-by-nine-foot room with an iron bunkbed nailed to the wall and a one-piece stainless-steel toilet and sink. It was dirty and smelled like sewage. For many weeks I did not speak to anyone or see daylight.

The lawyer came by to see me, and he had the same cold look in his eyes that the female deputy who had strip-searched me at the Oklahoma holding facility had. He told me I should plead guilty, and he would try to get me a prison sentence of ten years, but there were no guarantees.

"Ten years, for what?" I asked.

He told me that because of the scope of the drug ring, spanning several states, and the fact that I and most of those involved in the case were from New York City, the Virginia legal system was going to throw the book at us just to make a statement. I was in disbelief. *This just couldn't be. All this for being with a guy who was a drug dealer.* I would wrestle with this thought throughout my early years in prison.

I had time on my hands, so I did a lot of thinking. I thought about my situation, and the more I thought, the angrier I became. I sat in that jail cell for many weeks thinking back on my childhood. I thought about sharing a living space with my aunt and her six children, knowing that it was not my home. I thought about my mother having to leave her three children in Jamaica to go to a foreign land to try and make a life for them because their father decided to walk away—leaving me and my siblings fatherless. I thought about me, as a child, longing for the day I would finally meet my mother, only for that meeting to disappoint.

As I thought, I cried. My tears were tears of anger building and growing inside my empty soul. I was reminded of the drug dealers at various corners in my neighborhood and the dirty needles and crack pipes in my schoolyard. As I thought about the consequences of drugs, I remembered the drug that would rob my brother of his future at fifteen years old. I thought about the various forms of abuse I had experienced throughout my life.

My heart almost stopped beating when I wondered who was protecting my child as I sat in a cell that looked and smelled like a pit of death. Who was making sure she didn't go through what I had experienced throughout my life? The more I thought, the more the thoughts fueled my anger, which then turned to hate.

My hate wasn't focused on what had been done to me, nor was it directed toward a particular person. My hate was internal. I hated myself. I hated my existence. I was disappointed with myself for experiencing the life I had experienced and my inability to do something about it. I hated myself for being helpless and not achieving my dreams. Then I hated myself for dreaming of a life that was never attainable to begin with. If life hadn't already been a huge letdown, now I was stuck in a cell facing twenty-five years for a crime I hadn't committed.

I was filled with hate, and all sense of hope was overpowered by my anger. It was on this day I started to die in prison. I sank deeper and deeper into pain, suffering, depression, and hate.

After several months of going back and forth to court, the case was now considered a high-profile case. It was on the news and in the local papers. The detectives started to bring in everyone for questioning, even those who had nothing to do with the case. They brought in neighbors and childhood friends, as well as family members of those who were hauled in for questioning.

People were being picked up from their homes, schools, and workplaces. If suspects had dated anyone involved in the case, and they lived in Virginia, they were now under suspicion of being a coconspirator. Some were even arrested and thrown in jail without bail. Because of this, there were a lot of us being housed in the same county jail. Since they didn't want people from this high-profile case talking to each other or being threatened by one another, they began dispersing those involved in the case to various county jails around the Washington, DC, and Virginia area.

The county jail where they would transport me was on the outskirts of Virginia. It was a long drive from the jail where I had been. After about two hours of driving, we turned down a long, dusty back road to get to the jail. It looked like they had built the jail in the middle of the woods.

By this time, I was so angry and filled with hate that it didn't matter to me where they were taking me or what they did to me. I already felt death within my soul. I arrived at the heavily guarded jail where I would spend a little over one year of my imprisonment.

This jail was a little bigger than the jail I had come from. It had thick gray cement walls and automatic iron doors, and there were jail guards everywhere. The guards wore blue, starched uniforms and black, shiny shoes. But what I remember even more than their attire was their expressionless faces. It seemed as if they never blinked an eye and stared as if I was not human. They would only refer to me by my last name and inmate number.

Upon my arrival, I was strip-searched, with a partial internal-cavity search to make sure I was not smuggling anything in my body into their jail. I obliged without any emotion.

There was a female deputy who kept her eyes on me from the time I arrived at the jail. She stood out to me from the other jail guards because, while she wore the same uniform and badge, her stare was somewhat warm. She had a different approach from the other guards. While I did notice the slight difference, I remained indifferent to it. God would show me later that this woman was his instrument to be used in my life during the time I would be imprisoned at this jail.

I later found out that this guard's name was Ms. Jackson. She would stop by my cell at least twice a day to check on me and offer me an *Our Daily Bread* devotional book, even though I would not acknowledge her presence at my cell door. In my mind, she and everyone in that jail were nonexistent.

I only came out of my cell to shower, sometimes eat, get mail, see my lawyer, or go to court. My skin became pale from lack of exposure to sunlight. My days were spent alone with my gloomy thoughts as I stared at the ceiling. Any good thoughts were buried under years of old pain layered under my new pain.

One day, though, something unexpected happened. My name had been called for mail. When I got up from my bed, I saw that Ms. Jackson was handing out the mail. As she handed me my mail, she leaned into my ear and said, "Baby girl, God told me He has a plan for you."

I was annoyed, pretended to not hear her, and gave her an evil if-looks-could-strangle stare before quickly turning away. I was annoyed by this woman because if God was real, then I figured He—like everyone else—had abandoned me. Yet, I was quickly re-minded of years before when a taxi driver had kidnapped and aban-doned me at the age of twelve.

I was returning home from a visit to a friend in the suburbs of New Jersey. Another friend and I had traveled to the suburbs and back to Manhattan by Amtrak. When we arrived in Manhattan, my friend needed to travel one direction back to her Brooklyn home, and I needed to go another.

Instead of taking a local train back home, I decided to take a taxi from Manhattan to my Brooklyn address. While it was after 10:00 pm, it didn't take me long to flag a taxi and tell him where I was headed. He nodded for me to get in the car. After driving for about twenty minutes, he asked to be paid before getting to my home address. When I told him I didn't have the money but that my mother would pay him when we arrived at the destination, he did not believe me and became irate. He said I was trying to set him up to be robbed.

I told him I had just come from visiting my friend who moved to New Jersey and that I didn't have any money on me, but I promised him that my mother was waiting at home to pay him. I even offered to call at a public phone so he could speak with her. He didn't want to hear anything I said.

Suddenly, the driver started driving dangerously fast—too fast for me to jump out. He drove to an alley in the Meatpacking District of Manhattan (at the time I didn't know places like this existed in Manhattan) that was populated with drug addicts, prostitutes, and pimps. He then got out of the car and made his way around to my side of the car.

I cried and pleaded with him as he dragged me out of the car and threw me onto the pavement. I frantically assured him again that my mother was going to pay him, but he drove off with all my belongings, leaving me in what seemed like a world of death.

I stood in the darkness of the night, fear flooding my soul, while many eyes stared at me. I quickly walked over to a corner, sat on the ground, pulled my knees to my chest. lowered my head, and wept.

A few minutes later, a woman walked over to me and placed a jacket around me. She helped me up and walked me over to a cab. She paid the taxi driver and told him to take me where I needed to go. But before he pulled away, she knocked on my window. When I wound down the window, she stuck her head in and said, "Now, honey, God's got a plan for you. Don't let me see you around here again."

Now, hearing those same words again from the deputy took me back to that frightening night. Little did I know I was about to walk into another dark situation—not in the Meatpacking District of Manhattan but within myself.

The very next evening the same deputy called my name over the jail speaker system to come to the door and pick up my mail. Apparently, they had called me earlier that day to get my mail, but I was sleeping at the time. Upon receiving a large envelope, I turned away to head back to my cell.

As I was walking up the stairs toward my cell, I opened the envelope and noticed there were pictures. One was a picture taken of my daughter, whom I had not seen in a year. Something about the picture looked strange, and when I brought it closer to my eyes, my knees started to buckle. My daughter's face looked skinny, and her eyes looked hollow, sad, and weary.

I felt like I could barely breathe and as if the room was spinning. I needed desperately to get to my cell, but I could barely see the staircase or hold onto the bannister. To see the lifeless eyes of someone you gave birth to—someone you love with every ounce of your body—is heartrending. I wanted to scream but couldn't seem to find my vocal chords. I wanted to cry, but no tears could find their way to my tear ducts. I wanted to run but had nowhere to go. All I could see were walls through my blurred vision.

I tried again to make it to my cell, but it seemed like buried pain was trying to explode. As I tried to hold in my agitation, I heard a gutwrenching scream and realized the sound was coming from my throat as tears, anger, hate, and pain welled up. The next thing I remember is waking up in an unfamiliar room.

I was in a white, padded room lying on a green iron slab sticking out of the side of a wall. I felt cold, weak, and lifeless—except for a pounding headache. A doctor's voice came over the intercom and explained that I was being detained in the psychiatric ward under suicide watch. He explained that I had gone berserk in the common area after receiving my mail—crying and screaming uncontrollably, shouting, and violently pushing people. I had thrown Ms. Jackson to the ground when she tried to calm me and had then fallen, hit my head on the recreation table, and passed out.

My thoughts flashed back to the last thing I remembered: the picture of my daughter. I wished to die in that moment. My heart felt more pain than the knot that was on my head, and I refused to eat for the next several days. I stayed in that room on suicide watch for about two weeks until my eating regulated.

After being released back into the general population, I was escorted to my cell by the jail guards. There was a small table in my cell, and on that table were the pictures I had received. On top of the pictures was a note: "God is trying to reach you; open your heart, daughter." I tore that paper until I couldn't tear it anymore.

*What kind of God would allow me to go through this?* I thought to myself. I desperately wanted the crazy, stalking deputy lady to leave me alone. I stood staring at the pictures of my daughter, and I wept uncontrollably as I held Tenae's pictures close to my chest. I sobbed until I had lost my ability to stand and fell to the ground. I had no desire to ever get back up. Life was not worth living.

I would realize later that in that moment—and in moments of agony to come—God was stripping me of me. He was dealing with my soul. I had so much emotional and mental baggage that He had to work deep within the core of my being. This would be the beginning stages of God breaking into the calloused walls surrounding my heart.

Eventually, I fell asleep on the cold, cement floor clutching the pictures of my now three-year-old daughter. Something strange happened to me that night that I will never forget because my life has never been the same since. I was awoken a little after 3:00 a.m. by a bright light. I knew what time it was because there was a huge clock on the wall opposite my second-floor cell.

The intense light shined into my cell, and although I felt weak, I found the light calming and peaceful. I sat up on the floor and looked outside my locked cell door. The light was not shining from that direction; it was pitch dark out there. I turned around and realized the light was coming through a sliver of a window in my cell. The cell had a narrow, one-way window that allowed me to see shadowy figures outside and the striped parking lot, but no one from the outside could see in.

As I walked closer to the window, I could see that it was the moon that was shining intensely into my cell. I stood staring at the moon, and I felt a peace come over me that I cannot explain to this day. I could feel that my face was stiff from dried tears, but the warmth of this light on my face brought an overwhelming peace that seemed to soften the skin on my face.

The moon moved out of my sight, and I sat on the little iron-slab table, next to the window, trying to comprehend what I was feeling. I picked Tenae's picture off the floor and held it to my heart, and once more the tears began to stream down my face. The pain was unbearable. I felt my heart beat rapidly and a knot form in my stomach. I put my face in my hands and began to sob. Suddenly, the bright light filled my cell again.

I turned to stare out the window through my tears, and there was the moon again—directly facing me, in full view. It was as if the moon had moved backward to position itself right in front of the narrow window of my cell. I wiped my tears and stared intently, and then I heard an audible voice, as if a person were standing in the middle of that cell with me. The sound of the voice was peaceful and inviting and seemed to fill every space in my room. It wasn't coming from behind me or in front of me. It seemed as if it were coming from every direction at once.

"Nadine, give me three more years of your life in prison," I heard.

I had already been in jail for a little over a year, and the thought of three more years made me extremely sad. I looked at Tenae's picture, fell to my knees, and said, "I can't do any more years in here. I just can't do it!"

"I will take care of Tenae," the voice replied. "I need three more years with you in here." By now I was on the floor on my knees with my face in my hand, tears streaming down my face and forming a small puddle on my cell floor. Yet, I felt a warm, calming peace within me.

I sat in that presence not wanting to move, and in that peaceful silence, I heard myself say, "Yes...yes, I will give you three more years."

I don't know why I agreed, but I knew, without a doubt, it was God who was speaking to me. I didn't know what my "yes" meant, but I knew I was surrendering to something greater than myself. The peace that flooded the cell that morning is indescribable. I stayed on my knees that night for what seemed like hours as I was immersed in the presence of God.

My vocabulary is too limited to explain what happened on that winter morning. And maybe I am not supposed to be able to describe it, but to just let the experience be. When I finally got up from the floor and lay on the little bed, I experienced one of the best, most peaceful sleeps I have ever had to this day—in a prison cell, on an iron bed, with iron bars as my room door.

I don't remember eating that day. I stayed in my cell and mentally walked through the events that took place in the wee hours of that morning. I went to bed early that evening hoping God would visit me again, and He did visit me again but in a different way.

The following day Ms. Jackson walked in, radiating the same warmth I had felt from her on the day I arrived at that jail. This time I was waiting to greet her with a smile. She didn't say anything, but it was obvious she knew something had changed. She gave me a warm smile. I attempted to apologize for my actions a couple weeks back, but she only shook her head, as if to say "no need" and kept walking to do her rounds.

The next morning I was awakened suddenly at about 2:45 a.m. When I awoke I didn't have a bright, peaceful light shining in my room like my earlier experience. This time there was only a small light from the moon shining at the foot of my bed. When I looked at the light, I saw a book at the foot of my bed on top of my covers. I knew Ms. Jackson had placed it there when I saw the title. I grabbed the book and sat on the table by the narrow window where the moon was slightly shining into my cell, giving me enough light to see.

That night I read a book called *A Divine Revelation of Hell* by Mary K. Baxter. Now, I will not make any attempts to justify the theology of this book, since it speaks of details that aren't necessarily in the Bible, like the afterlife. However, midway into that book, I went on my knees on the hard, cement floor, in a cold cell, somewhere in a wooded area in a jail on the outskirts of Virginia and gave my life to the Lord.

That day in 1996 marked a pivotal turning point in my life. And God orchestrated that time line of events all by Himself. Far beyond the comforts of a church altar or beyond the preaching of a compelling sermon, God would use a series of circumstances and a prison cell to chip away at my calloused heart and lead me to a well that offered soul-satisfying water.

All my life I was thirsting for something but never knew what it was. I was trying to satisfy my inner thirst with things that would only leave me emptier and thirstier. This cycle increased my frustration as I kept pouring things down what seemed like a bottomless hole. *But God* met me exactly where I was: in the middle of my hurt, pain, sorrow, and hate. That morning I wept again, but this time I cried tears of joy, peace and freedom. Ironically, I felt a freedom in prison that I had never experienced when I was living in the free world.

I couldn't wait to see Ms. Jackson to tell her what happened to me as I read that book. I paced back and forth in my cell waiting for her to make her morning rounds. Like clockwork, she walked her rounds on the lower level and then made her way up to the second level where my cell was located. She stopped at my cell, and I could not contain the tears that were flowing onto my orange prison uniform. Through a river of tears and quivering words from my mouth, I told her of the things that had transpired in the wee hours of the morning and how God had used her in the process.

As a jail officer, she did her professional best to hold back her own tears, but after she left my cell, she returned with the greatest gift any human has ever given me: my first Bible. It was an average-looking blue Bible. But there was nothing average about what was inside. I read that book from cover to cover, taking in every passage, every story, and every lesson. It was as if someone had handed me the keys of my prison that day and told me to walk out into my freedom.

That day a new life had begun for me, and I had discovered freedom in prison—freedom within my soul. I was so imprisoned by hate, bitterness, anger, and years of buried pain that I didn't realize I had been barely living. I was simply existing. Then, unannounced, into my cell walked freedom to liberate me from my inner turmoil.

About two weeks after Ms. Jackson gave me the Bible, she was relocated to another jail in another city. On her last day at the jail, she stopped by my cell to say her final good-byes. She told me she believed she was sent to that jail just for me, and she told me she began praying for me the day I arrived. I was glad she had. I will never forget how God used her in my life to show me so much love and patience.

The Bible Ms. Jackson placed in my hands was like bread for the hungry and water for the thirsty. I still have that Bible today, and much of it is held together by tape and glue.

# CHAPTER 7

# The Freedom Within

*Out of suffering have emerged the strongest souls; the
most massive characters are seared with scars.*

—KHALIL GIBRAN, THE BROKEN WINGS

DURING MY EARLY YEARS OF incarceration, I spent a lot of time in
Virginia county jails. I would often see the same people come in and
out of jail. They would commit crimes, go to jail, go to court, be
released, and begin the process all over again, for months at a time.
Many of them were drug addicts who committed crimes to support
their drug addiction.

It bothered me that they were being given opportunities to go home
and be with their families and yet they kept coming back to jail.

Here I was not getting even one opportunity to go home and be with my daughter. I knew that given another chance, I would never reenter the jail system. I had found a new way of thinking and living. My life was changed. But God knew I wasn't ready to go beyond the boundaries of my physical prison walls. And deep down, as much as I hated to admit it to myself, I too knew I wasn't ready.

All my days and nights in prison were spent reading the Bible. I would read it from sun up to sun down. I would get up at three o'clock in the morning just to read and pray, and I would talk to God about everything. I talked to Him about the issues surrounding my birth. Why wasn't I wanted? Rejection is a very powerful thing that can permanently scar a life. I needed God to help me move beyond those scars.

Abuse was another deep wound that needed healing. My abuse was physical, emotional, and mental, and God had to help me see myself the way He sees me. My identity was not determined by what happened to me, and I was not what people said about me or thought of me, no matter the circumstance. I was not to blame for the painful actions of others. I had to learn to see myself through the love of God and find beauty among my ashes.

During this time, I had to go through a process of forgiveness so that true healing could take place at its deepest root. I learned that saying "I forgive you" doesn't make what people did to me right. Forgiveness says, "I will no longer be held captive by your actions." I gave myself permission to forgive and move forward, which was a process that brought healing and freedom to my own soul.

As I look back, it seemed as if something or someone was always out to get me. The details of rape in my younger years always chills my soul as I look back. Some situations I was able to get out of while, at other times, I was not so fortunate.

I mentioned earlier in this book that I was kidnapped by a man as a teenager and came across the same man while driving on a DC highway as a young adult. That kidnapping took place while going to school one day when I was fourteen years old, in one of New York's stormy winters. The walk from my house to the train station was a good distance. So, I would take the bus to the train station. On this particular day, due to the snowstorm, the bus was taking a very long time to arrive at my stop, and I had an exam that morning that I needed to take.

A nice-looking burgundy Lincoln Town Car pulled up, and a muscular Caucasian man in his late fifties offered to take me to the train station. I initially refused, but the gentleman said he was going in that direction and that the weather was too brutal for me to endure waiting for a bus which could take a long time to arrive.

I eventually agreed, and I attempted to get into the back seat; however, the man asked if I could sit in the front passenger seat so the police wouldn't think that he was running an illegal taxi service. So, I sat in the front. He made small talk in the beginning, and then about five minutes into the drive, I heard the car locks click; they could only be unlocked from the driver's side.

The man started yelling that my mother should have taught me not to get into cars with strangers and that he was going to teach me a lesson. I started saying to my fourteen year old self, "Nadine, just think and stay calm."

"Didn't your mother teach you not to get into cars with strangers?" he shouted.

*Something* told me to answer him unless he will become more enraged by my silence. And so, I said, "yes."

"Then, I will teach you a severe lesson of why you should always listen to your mother." Fear gripped my heart. This man was visibly angry and seemingly violent. Suddenly, a thought came to me, and I told him I had friends and that I could go and get them for him. He became really interested in what I was saying and asked me where my friends were. I told him they were at school and that I would get them and bring them with me to his house.

He told me I had better not be lying or else he would come find me since he knew which neighborhood I lived in. I assured him I was going to get at least three of my friends. He took me to where his high-rise apartment building was (not far from the train station) and told me what apartment he lived in—6D.

He unlocked the car, and I couldn't get out fast enough. I ran into the train station and sat on the floor in a corner and cried. I thought about the time the cab driver had dropped me off in an area in-fested by prostitution a couple years prior. I never made it to school that day, and unfortunately, I never reported it to the police or told anyone else what happened. I was paralyzed with fear and I blamed myself for what happened.

I do not know what would have happened to me that day if I had not lied to that man. After that incident, I did not leave my house for weeks, as I feared for my life. And as you've already read in a previous chapter, this was not my last encounter with this de-ranged man.

As I sat in jail, my mind would often drift to various painful expe-riences, and I couldn't help but notice how my life was always be-ing sought after by two worlds. One was a world of destruction and death, and the other world was always trying to save me from the destruction.

One day as I sat down in my cell reading my Bible, I heard the main doors open as the other women yelled, "New girl!" This was common when a new person entered the jail, but for some reason I did something I had never done before: I got up from my bed to see who the person was.

I saw a very pretty, tall young woman—probably in her early thirties—walk into the common area holding her bedding and jail toiletries. I caught myself staring intently at this new inmate. Something told me that she and I would end up being friends.

I later found out the woman's name was Linda, and she had two things going on in her life: she was a struggling crack addict (which was why she was in jail), and she had a strong calling of purpose on her life. Anyone who met Linda recognized the second point. I eventually learned that Linda had years of in-and-out history in that particular jail—she was something like her one hundredth time of incarceration. Yet, for some reason she seemed like a breath of fresh air when she walked into the jail.

Even though she was battling crack addiction, God still had His hand on her life. God saw her as a precious diamond with major struggles. She was in jail to protect her life from the drug that was trying to destroy it. God also allowed Linda to be there at the same time I was because he was going to use her in my life as Paul was used in Timothy's life. No human has had a greater impact in my spiritual journey than Linda Wellington, a struggling crack addict—especially in my early walk as a Christian.

Linda was assigned to be my cellmate. The entire time I had been in this jail, I had never had a roommate, but Linda would change that. It was as if that empty bed was waiting for her arrival. I remember hearing her pray for the first time, and it seemed like the prison itself shook. No wonder the enemy was out to destroy her life. Linda's Bible teaching came with power and authority, and she helped me understand the power of prayer. Today people call me a prayer warrior, but I shrink in comparison to Linda. She prayed the scriptures. Her prayers were that simple and yet so profound.

I remember asking her once to teach me how to pray. She told me her prayer life was birthed out of a life filled with much pain and travail. She told me she has had many defeats and regrets but also some victories in her life, and her prayer life was a result of that journey. One of her biggest problem in her years of battling addiction to crack was her husband—who not only introduced her to the drug but was also her supplier.

Linda was a small-town girl who went away to attend school at Norfolk University. She was nineteen when she met her soon-to-be-husband, who was thirty-eight. She became pregnant a few months after meeting him, and they were married five weeks later. However, not only was this man a small-time drug dealer, he was also a heavy crack user.

Just before Linda gave birth to her first child, she started smoking crack. Before her baby was one year old, Linda became addicted to this life-controlling substance, and her husband would readily supply what she needed to feed her habit. She went on to give birth to five children, and all of them were taken from her because they were born with drug-related health complications.

Linda and I prayed together and did Bible studies together. As we began to spend time in God's Word and have times of intentional prayer, I received consuming zeal and passion for God that was uncontainable. I wrote letters to everyone I knew telling them about the love of Christ that had freed me from the prison of sin. I had my family send me addresses of past friends and people I had not seen in years, and I would write letters to them describing God's love for them and His purposes for their lives.

Many of these people were shocked because this was not the Nadine they knew from my days of gang-related activities and my reckless lifestyle. They were all appreciative of those letters, though, and some have kept them to this day. I wanted everyone to experience the love I was experiencing and to know this love that cost absolutely nothing. I wrote many letters of forgiveness to those who had caused me much pain. I also wrote letters asking for forgiveness from those I had wronged and mistreated over the years.

I was going through a process of healing and did not know it. My healing was linked to me letting go and allowing God's freedom to flood the dark spaces within my soul. During this season of my life, I felt the weight of the world lift from my shoulders. The freedom I experienced during this time couldn't come through someone else; it had to be encountered up close and personal. I was being transformed from the inside out, and no prison bars could contain it or control it. It was powerful and liberating.

I couldn't read the Bible enough, even though I read it most of every day. Not only was I learning about God and His works within earthly creation, but I was also learning about His works within me. I was discovering who I was through God's eternal lens. I was learning about my identity and discovering the beauty beyond my scars. I was accepting the fact that my past and the pain I experienced from it would forever be a part of my life, but I would no longer be held captive to it. I was free indeed.

When I wasn't reading, I was talking to God. I would wake up and hear myself praying. I would pray for the guards as well as the inmates. I would write letters of prayers and mail them to friends and loved ones. The Bible had become my daily bread, and I couldn't get enough of it. The more I read, the more God was revealing Himself to me.

As unlikely as it seems, this was the greatest time of my life. I had experienced God as my Savior, but now I was experiencing Him as the lover of my soul as I would sense Him speaking to my heart. No human being could offer such love. I continued to grow in my faith, all while going back and forth to court and applying my faith, believing that God would send me home when it was time.

I had unmovable faith and trust in God's plans for my physical freedom, yet there was always a space within me that longed to go home and be with my daughter. Even though I found God's decision for me to remain in prison very difficult to swallow. I believed then and I still believe today, that in His love, God will give us what we need over what we want. Yes, I earnestly wanted to go home and be with my daughter, but God was working on something far greater, my inner freedom. I knew what I wanted but God knew what I needed.

God began working on my inner freedom before He started working on my physical freedom. Physical freedom was the easy part, but freeing me from the hurts of my past would take time and patience. I had layers of pain and hurt that needed to be peeled away, and it could not be done without my cooperation—the yielding of my will. I even yielded my will to go home, choosing to accept God's will even if it meant staying in prison longer than I desired.

This was not easy, but that decision had been the pivotal moment in my prison experience. God knew exactly when I would be ready to go out into the world and face the demons that awaited me. When I released control of my life to God's ultimate plans for my life, I began to see the purpose of my imprisonment. Prison wasn't meant to destroy me; God was using prison to develop me.

There were many mountains to climb and battles to fight, but the greatest battle was the battle of *self.* To my surprise there was still a lot of self that was in the way and hindering my growth. I was quick-tempered at times and gave others a piece of my Jesus-loving mind if they said something or did something I felt was not right or fair.

My lack of discipline in being slow to speak has caused me to say things I wish I could reverse. One of the ways God helped me work on my undisciplined tongue was by working on my thought processing. During this time, if I thought it, those around me heard it. Yet, too often my thoughts were negative and not constructive to the hearer. Oddly enough, once I surrendered it to

God, He would one day use the very area in my life that I used so negatively, to have a profound positive impact on many lives, my speech.

God challenged me to paste His truths about me around my entire cell. I found words in the Bible that were uplifting not only to myself but to others as well. My mind had to unlearn the lies that I had been raised to believe about myself.

Every day, I awoke to see words of life, self-worth, and positive affirmations around my cell—on the walls, by the sink, and on the mirror. Everywhere I looked, God had me tape words He desired to use to help build my self-image, my identity, my self-respect and His unconditional love for me. This was important because hurting people hurt people. They treat and respond to people from their place of hurt. But if God could heal that place of hurt and help me to see myself the way He sees me, then my response to people can come from a place of love and respect for them as well as myself.

I was going through a transformation and did not know it. I was following God out of obedience, not knowing that where it was taking me was more for my benefit than it was for God. Not only was this process helping how I thought about myself and others, but it also helped me relate to my surroundings in a healthy, positive way.

A kind and loving attitude and behavior is not normal in prison, and other inmates can view these traits as a sign of weakness— which can sometimes make you a target for physical attacks. But as I was learning who I was and who God was in me, I feared no evil. I was free to let God abide in me and through me. I started loving everyone, even those in prison that did not have my best in mind. But that didn't stop me from loving them anyway. This love I was experiencing wasn't mine to keep but mine to give, to the loving and the not so loving.

My spiritual boot camp was prison, and it would be a challenging and sometimes painful journey that would stretch and grow me beyond my comfort level. I learned that butterflies aren't born with wings; they must go through a developmental process. Prison, and the lessons I would learn while being there, would help me gain my wings. I didn't know it at the time but I would begin to fly in purpose right behind cinder blocks and metal bars.

CHAPTER 8

# A Change Is Coming

IN JULY OF 1997 MY day to be sentenced had finally come. I had
been in the county jail for almost two years, going back and forth
to court and now the day arrived that I would hear the fate of my
freedom. My lawyer had talked me into pleading guilty to the con-
spiracy charge since everything that was in my name was purchased
with money from drug sales. He also stated that the judge could give
me probation where I could be released to go home to my family. I
was reluctant but he said if I didn't plead guilty they would throw
the book at me and the next time I would see my daughter as a free
woman she would be an adult. I plead guilty. Before I left the jail to
head over to my sentencing, the ladies in the jail gathered around
my cell in anticipation that I would be released to go home that day.
Each requested something from my cell that I had accumulated over
the time I had been incarcerated. I told them it wasn't a guarantee
I would be released, so I couldn't give anything away yet. But they
thought for sure I would be released since I was just the girlfriend.

They stated over and over that the judge would see that I was not involved in Eric's affairs and give me probation or house arrest. One of them said, "I have done much worse than you could ever imagine and got caught red-handed, and each time I have been released with probation or house arrest, so you—my college-attending sister—are going home *today!*"

I remained quiet and stilled my heart. Only the Lord and I knew that it was on a cold winter morning at about three o'clock when I gave Him my word that I would give Him a few more years of devoting my life to Him in prison. And I meant it. But that was then. Now, the taste of physical freedom was so close, something inside me was whispering, *"Lord, would you release me from these bars today? Haven't I grown a lot since that day you spoke to me in my cell? I've stayed in the scriptures, built a prayer life, and I have control over my tongue now."*

As quickly as those whispering thoughts came, I would silence them. *No, Nadine, not my will but God's will be done.* It was an internal battle that lasted all morning as I prepared for the federal marshals to transport me to the main court in downtown Norfolk. My mouth felt dry as I knelt on the concrete floor next to my iron bed that was bolted to the wall. I prayed and asked God to be my judge and jury. I asked Him to go before me. But most importantly, I asked that His will would be accomplished and not mine, no matter what His will looked like nor the pain it would bring.

Deep down I knew God was not finished with me in prison. When I stood to my feet and turned around, two marshals were waiting with handcuffs in hand to transport me on a nearly two-hour drive to the courthouse. Upon entering the courtroom, I saw family, friends, and even college professors who had come to support me. Their presence spoke of their love and support for me.

My judge was over ninety years old and from the south. He wore a black robe and glasses that hung low from the bridge of his nose. His look was ice cold. He showed no facial expression as each character witness took the stand to speak on my behalf. He asked if I had anything to say, and I did. I spoke of my childhood and upbringing. But, ultimately, I told him I was prepared and would fully respect whatever decision the court made.

He sentenced me to five years and ten months in a federal prison in front of a courtroom filled with tears and sadness. Even the marshals were shocked at such a heavy sentence, but deep down, I wasn't surprised. I lifted my head, collected myself, and while the tears rolled down my face, I thanked the expressionless judge. The marshals then quickly removed me from the courtroom and drove me back to the jail.

I didn't talk on the drive back to the jail. Instead I thought, *The life I live is no longer mine but God's*. While we may have an inclination of the journey we are embarking on, we don't know the experiences we will encounter and the emotions those experiences will illicit along the way. I understood that from that moment on, my life was no longer in my hands or within my control; it was totally surrendered to God's will and His plans for me.

It is difficult, at times, not knowing where God's will and plans for you will take you. Embracing God's will, at times, is a difficult process yet one that brings liberation when we decide to let go of our control of life and fully trust it to God. Even when we don't understand. His plans for us far exceeds our plans for ourselves. But the issue of letting go and trusting God is a real battle for even the person with great faith.

The ladies in the county jail were waiting for me with great excitement when I returned from my sentencing. When I told them I wouldn't be going home anytime soon, their excitement came to a screeching halt, and they expressed their unbelief that God would allow me to receive such a gut-wrenching sentence. One of the younger ladies took my sentencing extremely hard. She said, "Why would God allow you to get more time than all of us put together and you love him so much, I just don't understand?" But it was actually in God's love that he kept me in prison as long as I needed to be there to prepare me for what He had for me. I explained to her that we often don't see what God sees. His viewpoint is macro and micro. It's macro because He sees my entire journey with one glance from a place that is high above my ability to see and know. Based on that advantageous view, He knows the best path for me. It's also micro because while He sees it from a view far above where I am, He also comes alongside me and walks with me in it and through it. He is in the everyday details of our lives along this journey called life.

My strength in God's unwavering faithfulness was already etched into my being. Nothing, not even a prison sentence, could move me to doubt or think any less of God. I knew, in the end, God would have the last say in my predicament and my life would be all the better for it.

I had already been in prison for two years now and was leading Bible studies. Linda, my prayer partner and sister in the faith, had long since been released, and just a few short months after her release, we received word that she died of a drug overdose as her two small children were visiting with her. The news was later substantiated when I wrote to her mother and received a letter back confirming the news of her death.

I wept bitterly for days. It was a huge loss for me. In spite of Linda's struggles, she was a woman I had come to admire for her faith in God. God used her instrumentally in my life, and the news of her death was news I would not understand for years to come.

In 1998 federal marshals airlifted me to another prison facility, where I would spend most of my prison sentence. I was placed in a maximum-security prison among a population of violent offenders, murderers, those who committed crimes using a gun, and those who were sentenced to spend the rest of their lives in prison.

I tried to tell the intake administrator that there had to be some mistake because I should be in the low-security facility. The low security facility was positioned on the same grounds of the maximum facility but on top of a hill with a short driving distance from each other. Those with non-violent crimes are usually sent there. This is why I was trying to explain to the intake administrator that since I had not been charged with a violent crime, I should be assigned to that facility. She looked up at me and said, "Sure, honey, that's what they all say. I'm sure you're about to tell me that you're innocent too, aren't you?"

*"Yea, but I am."* I thought to myself.

Even my lawyer told me I would be transported to a low-security facility, according to the paper work he had from the courts. At first I was frustrated by this confusion and this woman's attitude toward the situation but something told me to step back and let it play out. I told the lady, "ok and signed the intake paperwork that she placed in front of me." I didn't know what was before me but my heart was immediately filled with a sense of peace that *God's hand was in this.* I would come to see that from the first day I arrived in that prison, God had already gone ahead of me and prepared the way.

Sometimes what seems to be a negative situation playing against you is actually God setting up a play for you. So, I pulled back from trying to convince the intake administrator that I did not belong in the facility and paid close attention to what was taking place.

After the intake administrator practically laughed at me for telling her I was misclassified, she gave me a bag of prison toiletries and bedding. I was then marched single file, with a group of women, into a big, open yard where the general population was. It seemed like a scene from a movie.

All the inmates gathered around us yelling out who was going to take who to be their wives. Many of these women looked, acted, and talked like men. I thought to myself, *"You've got to be kidding me."*

While I was now a Christian and living the life of a Christian, I had not quite been delivered from the *old* Nadine just yet. I kept telling myself, *"If one of these females put a fingernail on me, they're going to have to send me to prison while I'm in prison."* Some of the inmates were getting closer to me, and my fists kept getting tighter and tighter.

As one of the big girls came to approach me, God intervened. I heard someone say, "Wait, is that Nadine?" I thought she must be talking about another Nadine because I didn't know anyone in prison. Again, I heard someone say, "Nadine, is that you?"

From left to right: My sister (Karen), brother (Gary), and I came to the United States in 1980. In this picture, we had been in the United States for just a few months. We were close in those days.

This was one of the highlights during my time in prison: getting to see and hold my daughter. Tenae was five years old in this picture.

On the weekends we were able to get dolled up, not to go anywhere but to take pictures. This allowed us to feel like we were more than a federal number. This picture was taken with one of the sisters in the prison.

My first Bible, given to me by Ms. Jackson, the jail deputy who introduced me to Jesus. The pages of this Bible are worn in use and filled with tears.

My family that God has blessed me with. From left to right: Me, Tenae, Isaiah, Natacia, and Bentz.

I turned and noticed a familiar face from when I was involved in gangs as a teenager. The woman grabbed me and hugged me while all the other ladies surrounding us, stared with eyes about to pop out of their heads. Yes, I did remember Keisha. I had saved her life in a Brooklyn train station many years before.

At the time I saved her life, I was with a well-known gang hanging out in a Brooklyn train station, up to no good. Several months before, Keisha had an altercation with one of the gang member's girlfriend. That altercation left the girl in a hospital room for days with broken ribs and a concussion. The boyfriend, who happened to be one of the main gang leaders, was seconds from pushing Keisha into an oncoming train when I pleaded with him to let her go because we were childhood friends. He did let her go, but not before giving her a beat down that caused her to have to remove her uterus. He kicked and stomped her in her stomach repetitively as she laid lifeless on the ground. Now, Keisha is about five feet three inches and 125 pounds, and this guy was about six feet four inches and easily 250 pounds. Keisha is a tough girl. She survived that brutal beating.

I had not seen her since then when she was released from the hospital which was years ago. And now here she was in the open yard of a federal maximum-security prison, where I just happened to be sentenced to do time. She kept yelling, "This girl saved my life! No one touches her, and anything she needs, she gets!"

Come to find out, Keisha was in prison for two murders, and she was one of the main leaders in the prison. From that day, I never had to worry about watching over my shoulders. Every meeting space I requested to do Bible studies or prayer meetings was cleared for me. When I needed extra Bibles for the ladies, Keisha made sure the prison administrators got them for me. I was given a smooth path because God used someone I knew from my past to clear a path in my present.

God knew exactly why He was putting me in maximum security. I didn't know it, but He had it all worked out for my good! The time I spent in that maximum-security facility allowed me to be a major influence in that prison as a Bible study teacher, facilitating various prayer groups, and even as a mentor.

There were a lot of young girls with hefty prison sentences who arrived scared and suicidal. The desire of my heart was to be there for them with support groups and a prayer net around them. Some would get lost in the harsh realities of the prison system, but others stayed close to the circles of care God was offering them.

After spending some time in that maximum-security facility and leading many different Bible groups, God transferred me into a low-security facility at the appropriate time. This facility had inmates who had lighter sentencing, and so they didn't stay long. Many didn't have time for Bible studies and prayer meetings. Their focus was on leaving—not trying to be comfortable while they were in prison. This impatient attitude filled them with anxiety and frustration. They wanted their time in prison to come to an end quickly so that they could go back to their previous lifestyles. But many did not leave when they thought they would, and because of this a lot of them suffered with depression and suicidal thoughts.

God would allow my influence from the maximum-security facility to follow me to this low-security camp facility. This worked in my favor for many reasons, but my influence also caused opposition from inmates and prison administrators.

# CHAPTER 9

# The Footmen

*On the darkest days when I feel inadequate,*

*unloved, and unworthy, I remember whose*

*daughter I am, and I straighten my crown!*

THE WARDEN IN THE LOW-SECURITY camp wasn't fond of my influence in her facility, and she made it known. She would withhold my mail. She would have the guards wake me up in the middle of the night to search my room. The guards would call my room to meals last. Time after time I was yanked out of the Bible studies and prayer meetings I was leading and placed in segregation on bogus charges. After a while it started weighing on me, and I wanted to give up—not on God but on doing His work in prison. But time would tell that God and His work go together like a baseball in a glove.

The last straw happened when my family brought my daughter to see me. I cherished visits from my daughter since I didn't get to see her much and had missed many milestones in her life, and my family had driven several hours from where they lived in New York to see me. However, when my family arrived, the guards told them they couldn't visit me, not even for a few minutes, even though they had traveled from another state to visit.

The guards claimed that my visiting privilege had been revoked for that day due to insubordination to an officer. They had made up this false accusation as soon as my family arrived in the visiting room. They escorted my family toward the door, with my daughter crying. I lost it and fell to the ground in tears. When my daughter turned around and saw me on the floor, she tried to run toward me, and the officer put out his hand to block her. She slipped and fell trying to avoid contact with his arm. No words could describe my hopelessness and brokenness as a mother. I just screamed out with a loud cry and said, "Why!!" I wasn't speaking to the guards but my anguish was toward God.

The memory of that day is like dagger in my heart. My hurt turned to fury when I was hauled off to segregation for attempting to assault an officer (this charge was later dropped because it was not true.) The enemy was trying to cut me down, piece by piece and in that moment, he was being successful.

One of the guards taking me to segregation admitted that the warden was making them harass me so I would stop doing Bible studies and holding prayer meetings in her prison. He told me it would only get worse, and it would continue to affect my visits with my family.

I was hurt and angry that God would allow these things to happen to me and not do anything. After all, I was being persecuted for what He placed in my heart to do. I went into a segregation cell (a small, cold room with a toilet and a sink and barely anything to eat) that reminded me of the hole-in-the-wall county jails that I thought I would never see the likes of again. I said to myself, *I will never teach another Bible study or lead another prayer meeting for the rest of my time in prison.*

At the maximum prison, we had close to five hundred women attending some of the Bible studies and prayer meetings. The new facility was much smaller, so we had fewer attendees, but these ladies looked forward to these times. I was angry, though. So, I told God to raise up someone else to do His work because I was not going to do it anymore.

My first day of being in segregation, a guard came by and slipped a Bible under my cell door. Segregation was in a section of the maximum-security facility where I had been previously, so a lot of those guards knew me. However, I didn't want God or His Bible. I was hurting and didn't feel like I could take it anymore. I cried, and my heart ached.

After I had sobbed for a short while, I heard the gentle whisper of the Holy Spirit ask, "Why are you angry?"

I replied, "Because you can deal with this lady and you won't."

All I heard was a still, small voice say, "Jeremiah twelve, five."

But I was too angry at God to read anything in the Bible. I fell asleep and awoke staring at the Bible on the floor in the corner. I went over to it and held it in my hand. Now perhaps I had read this scripture before (in fact, I'm certain I had), but as I read it, I did not recall ever coming across these particular verses. In my anger at God and my situation, I had felt I would never do another Bible study or prayer gathering again. But the moment I read Jeremiah 12:5 changed everything for the rest of my hardships in prison and how I would handle hardships for years to come. When God has handcrafted you for a purpose and His Word then speaks to that purpose, there is no escaping it—period.

That day, I didn't feel like I read the verse; I felt like the verse read me. It said: "If you have raced with men on foot and they have worn you out, how can you compete with horses? If you stumble in safe country, how will you manage in the thickets by the Jordan?" (NIV).

That verse stood me to my feet. You see, Jeremiah wanted to give up too. He was frustrated with evildoers and wanted to throw in the towel when God spoke these words to him. If the enemy can't get you to indulge in sin, he will try to discourage you from walking in God's will and plans for your life. He almost had me. But that verse turned everything around. I received a revelation while sitting in that segregation cell. And that was every guard that was assigned to frustrate me out of God's plans, they were trying to wear me out and tear me down emotionally, but they were all footmen! You see footmen can't halt God's plans for our lives but they can frustrate us and discourage us until we walk away from those plans. Now let me say, I've come across some wonderful human beings dressed in a prison guard uniform. They treated me with respect and dignity as they carried out their responsibilities as guards in federal prison. Their jobs aren't easy and at times very dangerous. I applaud them for the job they do on a day to day basis. But these particular guards were on assignment against me, taking strict orders from the warden.

I realize now that the enemy's tactics weren't the big stuff but little things sent to agitate me out of pursuing God's will for me: little things like, withholding my mail, denying my visits, and having guards shake my bed at night while I was asleep. The enemy was poking at my feelings, and God used Jeremiah 12:5 to awaken me and help me realize what type of battle I was in. When we understand the battle that we are in, it causes us to approach it from a different frame of mind. All battles are not the same. The strategy you used in one battle may look different from the one you need to use in another battle. This battle was after my confidence and courage to remain faithful in my current assignment. Giving up on Bible studies and prayer meetings was exactly what the enemy wanted me to do, and I was about to hand him what he wanted on a silver platter! After reading that verse, I stood up and asked God for forgiveness, locked and ready to continue my assignment.

I learned something else in segregation-no situation, no matter how bad it seems, is ever wasted by God. He will use the negative and turn it into a positive if we don't get in the way. Why do I say this? In segregation the cells are stacked to the right and left, and each level going up is stacked the same way. No inmate can see another inmate. Cells face a long hallway with an ugly steel-gray wall serving as a daily reminder that you're in prison.

The day God used Jeremiah 12:5 to strengthen me, I started singing "His Eye Is on the Sparrow" in my cell. Singing in segregation is not easy because the cells are filled with the noise of banging on cell bars, screaming, and loud crying. But that day

I started singing anyway. A young lady in the cell to my right asked if I could sing louder because her grandmother used to sing that song to her whenever her mom would leave her for a long period of time. So, I sang loud enough for her to hear. Then she joined in and started singing as well. The next thing I knew more and more of the ladies started singing until there was a symphony of voices.

Every morning, for days, we sang "His Eye Is on the Sparrow. The guards would run in and tell us to shut up. They feared unity because they thought unity could lead to rebellious rioting. But we would keep on singing, which silenced the screams of other inmates who were going through mental breakdowns. The more the guards told us to shut up, the more we sang to God. It was beautiful!

I used that time in segregation to pray and seek God for the strength and courage to do what He wanted me to do with the ladies who were waiting for my return. I prayed quietly, and I prayed allowed. I sang praises to God. Segregation would not silence the praises that were in me. God was proving to me more and more that he was with me, and just like I had been told many years before, He had a plan for my life. Now I was starting to understand. God showed me an opportunity for me to do Bible study with the young lady who was in the cell to my right. We couldn't see each other but who says you need to see each other to study the Bible together. I mean it would have been great but that wasn't our set-up so we made it work and God had a plan to use it! We were studying the life of Jesus based John's Gospel. While doing Bible studies with her for the days I was in segregation; the other ladies also asked the guards for a Bible so that they too could follow along in this Bible study. I would open in prayer, then go into the study, have reflection questions about what we read and then ask for any prayer requests as I closed in prayer. Very simple but they loved in and looked forward to our time at 7:00 pm.

The day before I left segregation, the young lady in the cell to my left asked if I would pray for her to receive Jesus into her heart. I had been praying aloud with her every night before she went to sleep be-cause she had terrible nightmares. I was blessed to lead her in prayer as she accepted Christ as her Lord and Savior. While leading her in this prayer, I could hear the ladies in the cells surrounding us, also praying. When we finished, I heard a unison of voices say, "Amen!"

I would have never had that opportunity had I not been in segrega-tion because several of those ladies were in prison serving life sen-tences and due to a riot many of them would be in segregation until they were transferred out to another prison. But God turned a nega-tive situation around by allowing me to be there to introduce them to a new life with Him. My life was not my own. It was in God's hands, and He had plans to use it for His glory, in His own way.

After eight days of being in segregation, I was released. As I was walking out of my cell, for the first time I saw the ladies in the cells to my right on the ground floor and above on the 2nd and 3rd floors who were doing the Bible studies with me. I looked up and around as they clapped for me and shouting their good-by. I was shocked to see that the majority of the women were Muslim, wearing their hijabs. They were Muslim women who had been part of a daily Bible study about the life of Christ and chosen to accept Christ into their hearts. Jesus comes to give life and freedom to everyone, regardless of our religious affiliations. I will never forget that experience. Immediately the guards walked me to the warden's office. I'll never forget how large it was. It had two big, bay-type windows. One overlooked the outside track area where inmates jogged or hung out during free time. The other overlooked the only long hallway that all inmates had to walk through to go anywhere outside of their rooms. I also noticed how minimally furnished the large office was. There was a large cherry business desk sitting between the two large windows, one executive-type chair—where the warden sat—and two smaller chairs.

I sat across from this imposing authority (she was about six feet four inches tall) looking at her bold blue eyes staring coldly at me through square lens. Her short blond hair was neatly cropped above her ears, and she wore a dark tailored suit. She stared for what seemed like hours. Even though I was five feet five inches and weighed 123 pounds and was wearing my orange prison jumpsuit with handcuffed wrists, I was not intimidated.

Finally, she aggressively leaned over her desk, pounded her finger into the desk, and said, "Now, you listen to me you little preacher woman. This is my last warning to you. You better stop preaching and praying in my prison or it will be painful until the day you leave."

I stared back at her, thinking, *Chile please, ain't nobody scared of you. You a footman in the grand scheme of things, and I'm not about to have you wear me out with your scare-tactic nonsense.* I responded, "No Bible studies and prayer meetings—which help these inmates and your prison...tell me, do you think that's a good idea?"

She leaned over that cherry table, again—this time closer to my face—telling me I was just another prisoner with a number. She then said furiously, "Listen here, whenever you are in your little God meetings, keep my name in the back of your mind!"

To which I responded in a respectful tone, "No, I'll keep you in the front of my mind, as I am always in prayer for *footman.*"

Her skin turned as red as could be. Then she yelled for the guards to escort me to my room and gave them strict orders that I was not allowed to leave my room for the next two days. While I was being escorted from her office, she yelled, "And I would have you know that I've been driving my own car since the age of fifteen!"

I laughed inside. It was clear she did not understand the footman comment. I confidently walked to my punishment with my head held high. I had a strong sense of God's protecting hedge over me, so I had nothing and no one to fear. After those two days, the ladies and I met in the recreation room to have Bible study, and after about two months, the warden was removed from the prison and another female warden took her place. I did not rejoice over this as other inmates did. I remained focus on sharing God's Word and His love with inmates that were in prison who were broken, discouraged and suicidal.

The new warden and I had a great relationship. She was pleased with what God was doing in the prison through the Bible studies and prayer gatherings, and she accommodated every request we had. She would often come to the Bible studies and sit in for about ten minutes every week. Before I left, she asked me to write her wedding vows, and I gladly wrote them based on 1 Corinthians 13.

Although I missed my family, especially my daughter, my time at this prison was needed. God would strengthen my faith in Him during this time. The disciplines of prayer, fasting, and countless hours in the Bible were a foundation that my faith would grow upon and rest upon to this very day.

Prison also had times of much laughter. So many different personalities are represented in prison that keeps the atmosphere full of activity. I remember once at the low-security facility on a beautiful but hot Saturday afternoon. A lot of us were outside sitting on the grass, talking and enjoying the view. Where we were sitting, we had a mountain view as you looked further out and just below us was a track for running. I would go out there to run and pray, often. A friend of ours, who had a quirky, awkwardly funny personality was on the track. What stood out to us is that she was dressed fully in a thick, grey sweatsuit and a towel wrapped around her neck. Now this would be fine if it wasn't for the fact that it was at least close to 90 degrees outside. She went around the track several times and each time she would look up at us and smile exuberantly. We all waived back with a bit of concern. Her last lap she decided to run. We all looked and thought to ourselves, okay darling, do you. One of the ladies who is extremely sarcastic said, "look at this fool!" Everyone burst out in laughter. She meant it in a loving way. You had to know her to understand. After our friend on the track finished her lap she then began to make her trek up the hill to where we were all seated. Now this was a pretty steep hill but she was determined to not walk up the hill but to run up the hill. When she got to where we were sitting she started looking at us but then said she couldn't see us and started yelling, "where is everyone, it's black, did the sun go out?" Our sarcastic friend once again with her sarcasm says, "no but you about to go out!" Before she could finish our exuberant track star was on the ground, passed out. We all ran over to her, terrified as we tried getting her up. Someone threw water on her face and she opened her eyes. She then started shaking her head from left to right, dramatically with heavy breathing and said, "where am I, where am I?" To which our sarcastic friend, who was in the back the entire time, jumped on the ground in the face of our lightly conscious friend and said with a loud voice, "you're in prison Dorothy!!" We all lost it. We were in stiches laughing so hard. My track star friend was fine but we didn't allow her to live that one down for a long time. We would click our heels together like Dorothy from the Wizard of Oz. Even some of the prison guards joined in on the joke. But this friend of mine had a great personality and would often laugh at herself.

I met many strong women of faith in prison—some who will never see the free world, as we know it, yet they are freer than many I've met in the free world. They have found their place in Christ no matter where they are geographically. I am forever blessed to have crossed paths with these women of great love and faith in God.

I endured many struggles and battles in prison, but they pale in comparison to what I gained. I found wings in prison that no prison walls could ever contain. In prison, I gave my life fully to Christ as His vessel and as a servant to countless women. God even gave me opportunities to witness to guards and wardens. They would share personal struggles with me in hopes of a word of comfort and direction from God's Word.

After some time I started a prison newsletter called *Moms Behind Bars* to encourage mothers like myself who were locked up and far away from their children. Of all the things I had to endure, being away from my daughter was my most difficult test. The newsletters were written to encourage mothers like me who had to walk through the pain of being separated from their children. I found healing and strength for myself as I was allowing myself to be used as a tool of encouragement for others.

When God calls us to surrender, he wants all of us—even the things we hold most dear. I've come to learn that what I could offer my daughter failed in comparison to what God could give her in my absence. My abilities are limited, but God's abilities are limitless. My love only goes so far, but He is the lover of her soul. While I can give her water and she will thirst again, He offers her living water she can drink and never thirst again. I had to release her into His ever-loving arms and trust that God is her safety and is able to sustain her no matter the odds. This trust in God gave me peace to move forward even when I didn't understand, and this is an ongoing lesson.

God would continue to work not just *with* me but also *in* me. There was still a lot of pruning and character molding God needed me to submit to. While I knew the Word, I had to continue to experience it in my everyday life—actively applying it and walking it out daily, even under harsh circumstances. God's character needed to replace my own, and it would be painful because someone had to die, and it wouldn't be God.

Sometimes the journey of transformation isn't about *becoming* anything. At times, it's simply about *unbecoming* everything that isn't really you, so that you can embrace and be who you were created to be in the first place.

It's startling when God allows you to look at yourself through His mirror. Man's mirror may view and applaud physical appearance, degrees, and eloquent speeches; but God's mirror views the deep corridors of our heart and sees the areas that need work.

God was showing me there were things in me I had picked up along the way that were harmful to me and would cost me greatly if I didn't truly face them and stop trying to cover them up with scripture quotes. Self-inventory isn't easy, but it's helpful when you know your areas of spiritual, emotional, and mental deficiencies. When we give God room to perfect our weaknesses, He gives us His best for our worst. It's a great exchange but one that is not forced, only offered.

We often have a way of hiding behind the exterior things that look and sound good while we are broken on the inside, leaving people to applaud our public life while our private life is a mess. God desires to work in these private areas within us, but far too often we mask them with exterior cover-ups like nice clothes, big homes, degrees, and even church attendance. But God is not impressed with our actions, He is impressed with our hearts: who we are beyond what the naked eye can see. We spend our lives trying to impress God and people with what we do, but God is looking for who we are and who we are becoming in Him.

Deep down, Nadine still had too much control to be totally used of God. He needed to strip me further of myself so I was not competing with Him. It takes teamwork to walk with God, and that would only come when I surrendered to the team leader, God Himself. I had to surrender then, and I am still surrendering today, daily.

# CHAPTER 10

# No Turning Back

*I guess we are who we are for a lot of reasons. And*
*maybe we'll never know all of them. But even if we*
*don't have the power to choose where we come from,*
*we can still choose where we go from there.*

—*The Perks of Being a Wallflower*

PRISON IS A SOCIETY IN and of itself, and corruption is a big part of that society. There are drugs, violence, rape, pregnancies, racism, cults, and gangs. If it's corrupt, prison has it.

There were clusters of communities in prison, and each community had its own set of leaders. Some of these leaders had more influence and power than the actual prison guards. It is very easy to get pulled into the prison mentality no matter how hard you try not to.

Almost everyone in prison wants to belong to something, and prison does not offer a plethora of positive options to choose from. Maintaining a walk with God in that kind of godless environment is extremely difficult—almost impossible.

I've been asked how was it that I did not get caught up in the prison mentality after being there for years. I believe what helped me were the principles and values I adopted after turning my life over to God. My values were based on God's Word, which told me that I mattered and so did my life. I saw what choosing the prison lifestyle looked like, and, I was worth more than that.

Prison was a pit stop—not my final destination. Therefore, I wasn't going to build a house where I was meant to build a tent. A house mentality meant I planned on making a home out of the prison system. But a tent mentality meant I was just passing through and had no intention on staying, mentally speaking. Now, keeping that mind-set wasn't always easy. I was living in an environment—every day, for years—that was the opposite of the direction I was going. I constantly reminded myself, "I may be in it, but I will not be of it. This part of my life is not a period, only a comma." Once you know where you're going, you will never be satisfied with where you are. The prison mentality and culture could not satisfy the woman I was becoming on the inside.

After experiencing many trials and even more victories, my day to be released from prison had come. I was ready but also unclear of the road that awaited me. I knew my time had come one glorious day when they called my name over the loudspeaker. I walked into the head administrator's office, who reported to the warden. He was not liked, and he liked it that way.

There were a lot of sexual relationships between inmates and prison guards, which was an automatic two-year federal prison sentence for the guard, if caught. Far too many times I would see a prison guard, and then suddenly he was gone for a little while. Later we would hear that an inmate was now impregnated.

Therefore, this administrator was emotionally cold as ice to avoid sexual temptations. I respected him, and he respected me. Plus, I saw another side of him. I could tell he drank a lot, and I would often find myself praying for him. Each time I would ask if he needed specific prayer for anything, he would respond, "Now, don't come bringing that jailhouse religion stuff to me. Keep that for these prisoners. They need it more than me." But I knew he needed prayer as much as the female inmates that populated the prison he was tasked with overseeing.

That day he called me to his office for the last time. As I was leaving, he said in a respectful tone, "you're free." To which I responded, "I had already been freed." He stared at me for a while with a smirk on his face and then said, "You know what? You're different. You won't be coming back."

"I sure won't!" I replied.

I entered the prison system in 1995 on a cold winter morning and left almost five years later on a beautiful spring afternoon. As I walked down a winding hill to the main building, I heard the Lord say to me, "He that thinks he stands, let him take heed unless he falls." I knew that was a warning, but I didn't know it was for me.

I was so glad to finally leave prison, to be free from prison guards and scheduled meals and working eight-hour days for six cents an hour. Yet, my heart was heavy for the sisters I was leaving behind. I prayed for these women as I walked into my physical freedom. Even though my heart was heavy, what gave me peace is that these women were living totally free, in prison. Freedom is more than your physical location, it is your state of mind. I too had found freedom long before I walked out of that prison. God had already set me free from my past, guilt, shame and feelings of insignificance. He had prepared me for where He was taking me. I walked out beyond those green, iron clad doors with something that was far greater than my felony record, I walked out with purpose. I didn't wait for anyone to pick me up or meet me at the train station. I sat quietly on an Amtrak in deep thought as tears streamed down my face. I had thought this day would never come, and now that it had, I didn't know what emotions to embrace.

I went into the prison system as a young, lost and broken girl, and now I was leaving whole and restored—forever changed. I had experienced wounds, but now I embraced the beauty in my scars. My tomorrow was dripping in purpose.

The prison I had once called a detour was actually a road called destiny. One of God's great acts is when He reaches down into the muck and mire of a person's life and brings that person who was far off, near to Himself, loving that person into a totally new person. His love for us, when received and embraced, totally changes us. His love is not afraid to go into our mess and scandal. His love chooses those whom society has rejected and marked as unworthy or unlovely.

This is a true love story—a story that depicts the great extent that God goes to reach the object of His love. And this He does even while the object of His love rejects Him time and time again. My praise and passion comes from that understanding. God's love met me where my soul was hurting, wrapped in pain, rejection and hate.

When I took hold of God's love and applied it to my hurt and barren soul, I began to live.

You see, prison for most of us is not physical iron bars and concrete cells. It's being held captive to past abuse, hurt, and emotional pain that we can't escape. Prison is destructive thought patterns and addictive behaviors that we can't seem to overcome. Prison is chronic thoughts of hopelessness or a poor sense of self-worth.

You don't have to be in a cell wearing an orange jumpsuit to be in prison. You can be imprisoned by your thoughts and emotions all while living in the free world, coming and going as you please, but being held captive by the circumstances of life, or incarcerated by the words of others. No one else could provide to me the prescription to the aching sickness that was deep within my soul, except God. His prescription of love and acceptance gave me a new identity.

The first person I saw after being released from prison was my mother. Even though our relationship had been strained for many years, while in prison I surrendered the pain and the hurt to God. I could not carry it any longer; it was suffocating me. The longer I nursed the pain and offense, the longer I remained stuck in the cycle of reliving many painful experiences that happened to me while I was growing up.

At first it was hard to let go of the hurt when I looked around at the prison bars, but unforgiveness was keeping me chained tighter than the physical bars around me. The deeply rooted bitterness was robbing me of life. I decided that letting go, no matter how difficult, was more beneficial to my wellbeing than staying chained.

While in prison I wrote my mother many letters to convey my gratitude and love to her for doing the best she could with what she had. That was a big part of my healing. I no longer sought to blame anyone for what went wrong in my life. Instead, I accepted that life happens to everyone. Some things that happen are good, while others are not so good. Some things are downright painful, but it was my choice to live and remain in the pain or accept it and move on from it.

We don't always have the power to choose what happens to us in life, but we can choose how we allow those things to mark us for better or worse. I made a firm decision to believe that I am not what happened to me. When I made that conscious decision, I was no longer a victim. I took the step of moving forward and pressing past the things that caused me many years of pain. It doesn't mean those things did not happen. It just meant I was no longer imprisoned by them. I was free. In that freedom, I received forgiveness, but I was also able to extend forgiveness.

When I went home from prison, my mother was there waiting with wide-open arms of love. My stepfather, Claude—my Pops—was there as well. He has always been there for me from the time he and my mother met, and his love for me has always been unconditional.

The second person I saw when I arrived home in New York was my sweet, seven-year-old daughter, Tenae. Of all the thoughts I had while serving time in prison, the one I thought of most was the day I would be reunited with my daughter. Oh, the joy! Nothing filled my heart more than seeing and kissing her pretty, little face. She was taller than the last time I had seen her in the prison.

She jumped into my arms, and I refused to stop hugging her. I cried, and so did she. We would be together again at last after all these years. Many times in prison when I felt like giving up and losing my mind—especially in the beginning—her face is what kept me going.

Tenae's personality is big enough to fill any room. Those times I would get to see her during a brief prison visit would bring me joy and encouragement to keep pushing ahead. I would tell myself, *You may not have anyone else, but you have a daughter who is waiting for her mommy to come home.* And now I was holding her in my arms; it was surreal.

Tenae originally thought I was away at school the entire time, and so she said, "Mommy, are you finished with school now?"

"Yes, Mommy is finished with school now," I sobbed.

# CHAPTER 11

# It's a New Beginning

*When I look back and see God's sustaining power, His*
*mercy, His love that endures, His faithfulness, His*
*provisions and protection, His peace, His victories in*
*the face of many trials, and then His saving grace, there*
*is a word that continues to fill my heart: grateful!*

LIFE IN THE FREE WORLD was different. I had been in prison for several years, and a lot in my city had changed. I had a lot of catching up to do, all while living in fast-paced New York City. I felt alone in what seemed to be a strange land that I had once called home. The transit system had changed. The style of clothing had changed. And I was clearly behind and not up with the changes. For instance, tokens and coins were no longer being used as access to transit transportation. I now needed a metro card. I was absolutely, clueless. No one told me this until one day, I had to shamefully exit a bus because I didn't have what I needed to gain access to the bus.

Some days I missed the strength and friendship of the sisters I had left behind in prison. My thoughts would often go to the times we would cry together, pray together, and support one another. Those ladies would risk their own comfort by standing up to the prison guards who were mistreating me. We were like family. Now, being back in New York I felt like a foreigner in the city I was raised in. Things felt different. I felt different. Relationships were different.

Don't get me wrong, New York is a beautiful place. It bustles with life twenty-four hours a day. It's the city that never sleeps. It's eclectic with many nationalities and people groups. I love the seasons, even though I could do without the scorching-hot summers and brutally cold winters. When New Yorkers visit other states, we say that we are from New York with a sense of pride… and sometimes arrogance. New Yorkers have a language of our own. The way we pronounce our words make us easy to identify in a crowded, chattering room. We have a style and culture of our own.

While I loved all of this about my hometown, New York also had a lot of memories attached to it, and I wanted to go somewhere else to start a new chapter. There were old friends who wanted to pick up where we left off, but instead they met a new Nadine with a sense of purpose and identity. The new Nadine didn't work for their lifestyle choices. The new me also placed a strain on some past meaningful friendships as well. I chose to sever ties with some of those friends, yet I will forever carry them deep within my heart. Purpose will often dictate what you allow and don't allow into your life. It will also affect who you hold on to and who you must choose to let go of.

After obtaining a job at an insurance firm in New York, I began to take care of my daughter on my own and live the life of a single mother again. Even though I had a job, I still felt restless about remaining in New York. I felt that I needed to leave, but I didn't know where to go nor did I have the financial resources to travel.

A little less than a year after I was released from prison, I started feeling a strong desire to move to Florida where my sister and her family were living. One day I resigned from my job at the insurance firm, packed my few belongings, and hopped on a plane heading to Fort Lauderdale, Florida, with my daughter. I left the fast-paced city life of New York and settled down in tropical South Florida. After two weeks, I secured a job at a well-known hotel chain and started as a front desk clerk. Not too long afterward, I was promoted to the sales department, handling the sports and entertainment groups. In spite of my felony record, God again, had gone before me.

My life became very busy with working a full-time job and raising a child on my own, and I had underestimated the cost of being a single mother. Even though I was working hard, I was only making enough to cover my bills and pay my monthly restitution fees to the courts (a requirement stipulated as part of my release from prison). Life became a bit overwhelming, and my relationship with God began to suffer.

I had not found a church to attend, regularly, since leaving prison, and I felt as if I was slowly drifting. The pressures of life and expectations I placed on myself became stressful and difficult for me to shoulder on my own. While I was elated to be with my daughter, the pressure I was experiencing caused me to long for the days in prison when I had the support of the community of women around me. I felt alone in a big world.

I began to slowly slip away from God and make ungodly decisions. I was ashamed of where I was in my life. Then I was reminded of what God had said to me the day I was leaving prison: "He that thinks he stands, let him take heed unless he falls." I was falling fast.

It was right around this time that I was invited to a church by a young man who lived in the same condo complex where I was living. Actually, he had invited me numerous times, but I had ignored him. He would always stick church flyers on my car window, which was fine unless it rained and I had to scrape the flyer off my windshield.

One night after a day filled with multiple unforeseen mishaps, I was standing in the rain outside my old, used Acura Integra that refused to start. It was one of those days that "when it rains, it pours." Standing in that torrential downpour, I started feeling dark hopelessness and depression creeping into my thoughts.

I thought of my prison years when my current responsibilities were not things I had to be concerned with—no rent, no bills, no single parenting, and no broken-down cars in the rain. The tears and the rain were both rolling down my face when the young gentlemen who always invited me to church drove up and asked if he could help. I found myself agreeing, begrudgingly, while feeling annoyed at his interruption of my depressing thoughts.

Then the man had the audacity to say he would only help if I would go to church that night. *You have got to be kidding me*, I thought. But before I could give him a snappy response, he jumped out of his car, looked under the hood of my car, and told me what the issue was. He said he had a friend who could fix the problem for me free of charge since he owed him a favor. Then he offered to take me and my daughter to church that night.

I took him up on the offer and attended that Wednesday night. There was some wonderful people who lovingly prayed for me after the service ended. I cried for what seemed like hours. They stayed as long as it took for me to get it all out of me. Some of these people are still in my life to this day.

That was seventeen years ago, and I've been attending Christian Life Center Church ever since. I've also been blessed with opportunities to serve in a plethora of ministries—from kids to youth to community outreach and, my favorite for obvious reasons, the prison ministry. While serving in the prison ministry, I learned the power of sharing our stories to bring hope and inspiration to the hearers. I was able to go into various prisons and local jails to share my story and encourage women who were in situations that I understood firsthand.

Eventually, I left my thriving job at the hotel and took a position in the church. Remember, once you've had the pull of where you're going you'll never be satisfied with where you are! God was ordering my steps just as He had promised. That one decision to leave the thriving position at the hotel and take the position at the church has altered the course of my life. I thought I was saying yes to a job, I would find out years later that I was saying yes to my call.

The gentlemen who introduced me to this amazing church community passed away a few years ago. I was privileged to speak at his funeral, and I shared the story of how he came to my rescue on a night when I felt discouraged, standing outside of a broken-down car in the rain many years before. I am forever grateful that he did not give up on inviting me to his church when I was struggling spiritually and had no one to turn to. I believe God sent him into my life at the right time for a divine purpose.

In 2003 God would again orchestrate a mighty move in my life. He would use one of my best friends, Tonya, to reunite me with my high-school sweetheart who she had introduced me to back in high school. I mentioned about this relationship earlier in this book. In high school this young man treated me with such dignity, love, and respect back when my life was filled with tumultuous storms.

One day, out of the blue, I received a phone call from Tonya, who was still living in New York City. She was inquiring about Bentz, from high school. I told her I knew nothing of his whereabouts. In fact, the last time I had seen him was when we broke up in high school. She told me that she heard he lived in Pennsylvania and that she would do a search to try and find him. I was a little surprised at her sudden desire to try and find him.

Tonya is a lawyer, so she has an investigative mind. I said ok, but I didn't care one way or another. I was living a fulfilling life serving in various ministries and raising my daughter as a single mother.

Tenae and I didn't have much, but we were together, and I was at a good place in life.

About a week later, Tonya called me back to tell me she had found two individuals in Pennsylvania with the name she was searching for and had contacted both of them. When she called the first number, she got a man's voice mail, and the other number just kept ringing. I immediately knew the second number was Bentz's. Bentz has never been a talkative person, so voice mail on his home phone is not a priority.

Tonya kept calling, and one day Bentz answered! He couldn't believe his high-school friend was on the other line. The first person he asked Tonya about was me. She gave him my number, and we talked everyday for about six months. No romantic interest, we were just old friends catching up on lost times. While I was in prison he heard of it through street talk and so he asked me about what led to that and what was that experience like for me. As months went on, and countless time spent on the phone, romantic feelings for each other began to develop. I took a trip to New York and he came to get me from the airport. The way he treated me during that trip was the same way he treated me in high school, with respect and dignity. Eight months into our renewed relationship, he told me that I would be his wife one day. I laughed.

Bentz eventually told me how odd it was that Tonya was able to reach him on that line. It turns out the line she called was not for a home phone at all. It was a line for Internet access. One day Bentz came home and his Internet wasn't working, so he went to a local convenient store and purchased a cheap landline phone to test the jack to see where the problem was coming from. When he plugged in the phone, it rang and kept on ringing because it had no voice mail set up. He answered it, annoyed, thinking it was a telemarketer, only to hear the voice of his dear friend from high school. Bentz and I were married almost a year after that first phone call. Not too long after we got married, we had two kids within seventeen months of each other. At the time of this writing, Isaiah is thirteen and Natacia is eleven.

A wise woman once told me, "Nadine, you have such a strong calling on your life that if the enemy can't get you to walk away from God, he will send you someone to marry who will frustrate God's call on your life." I almost made that dreadful mistake by marrying a person I met in New York while working for the insurance company. I would later come to realize he was an assignment from the pit of hell. But at the right time, God saved me from that grave mistake. All the while He knew He had already set apart a man for me in His timing. This man would be everything I had desired in a man and more.

I don't think I would be where I am in ministry without the love and support of my husband and best friend, Bentz. I have great supporters in my family and close friends, but there is nothing like the support of a spouse. The covering and security he brings into my life as a leader is immeasurable. I thank God every day for the husband and the father he is.

We are a team. We serve together. We mentor together. We make sacrifices together. And we laugh together. I could not ask for anything more. What I was looking for in a man, God exceeded. You don't really know the things you will need in a husband until you are married and you start walking through turbulent storms and facing major trials together. It is then you come to know the necessary ingredients needed to navigate the various potholes marriages so often face.

I used to wonder who could love me with such deep scars? Little did I know, God had already chosen someone!

*You will be a crown of splendor in the Lord's hand,*
*a royal diadem in the hand of your God.*

*—ISAIAH 62:3 (NIV)*

CHAPTER 12

# Purpose: A Journey, not a Destination

*How one chapter ends does not dictate the outcome of the book. A bad chapter doesn't have to be the end of story. It means you need to keep writing and change the narrative.*

THERE ARE TIMES WE GET to see the hand of God in our difficult circumstances and trials. We get to see God bring great and amazing things from lives filled with dark and challenging situations. I've had front-row seating to these type of God moves—not only in my own life but in the lives of many others. But truth be told, there are also times when God seems silent, and, quite frankly, you see more of the challenge than you see of His hand.

I've experienced these seasons of life more often than I've desired. It is in these moments I've learned that just because you can't see it doesn't mean God isn't working. I've also realized that when I've complained about not seeing God in my difficult circumstances it wasn't because He wasn't there but—honestly—He wasn't doing it the way I wanted Him to do it.

Many times, unbeknownst to me, God was very present, but I was so focused on the tumultuous waves that I missed the One who was standing on the water. So often I've overlooked that God was there guiding me through every hardship all along—leading me through it, not keeping me in it.

The quiet guidance of God has showed up for me in more ways than I can count. It showed up for me as a preteen in the dark allies of the Meat Packing District of New York City, as God would send a prostitute to stand in the gap for my protection. This, dormant yet intentional guidance of God showed up for me in an elementary school, during an abusive time of my life, in the form of a caring, nurturing fifth-grade teacher. This silent presence was there on a cold winter day in Brooklyn when I sat in a Lincoln Town Car with a deranged kidnapper. This ever present, yet sometimes undetected, guidance was there when I was thrown from a speeding car onto the Chesapeake Bay Bridge. It was there in a house where everyone was killed just hours after I left with my toddler.

God's guidance would accompany me to a jail, hidden on the out-skirts of Virginia, when a prison guard refused to give up on telling me about a love that was greater than my pain. It would show itself years later in a federal maximum-security prison when a childhood friend—who just happened to be in the prison I was sentenced to and who happened to be the main leader in the prison—not only intervened and stopped me from being assaulted but used her le-verage to grant me influence on my very first day in that prison.

God's presence would lead me out of terrifying situations time and time again, more times than the pages of this book would allow me to share. God's presence and guidance in my life have proven to be constant yet sometimes undetected in the moment. He was there all along, but I didn't notice Him. Many of these moments I would credit to luck or coincidence at the time. Yet, His love is so secure it didn't need to scream, "It's Me!" It just continued to show up, con-sistently—and many times, silently—knowing one day my blinded eyes would no longer be able to deny a love so rich and deep that it's too blatant to ignore.

People have asked me, "Why would God allow you to go through all the things you went through?" I think the answer is quite simple. Everything I went through served a greater purpose. I believe the experiences I went through, good and bad, helped shape who I am today. Many things I would not have chosen for my life but neither would I change it. The things I went through are what inspired me to write this book.

Whenever I look into the eyes of women, young and old, who are compromising themselves and feel little self-worth, I see myself before purpose found me. When I am privileged to speak with so many of these beautiful women who just aren't sure of their value, I don't speak from a place of condemnation but from a place of compassion because that woman staring back at me with tears in her eyes was once me.

I understand the pain of wanting to be free but not knowing how to get there, thinking this must be how things are supposed to be. I realize now that those years of turmoil weren't wasted years for me, as the results of those experiences now bring hope and healing to those who are in similar situations. This doesn't mean God sent those negative circumstances into my life, but he can heal me of them and certainly use them to help bring healing to someone else.

Sometimes the poor choices of others can impact our lives. But God can turn what was meant for evil into good. He can restore what has been broken and mend the pain we have experienced and use those things to help bring restoration to those who are hurting without a sense of hope. It is amazing to me that no story is so messed up that it's void of hope. God desires to bring hope to those who think their lives have no significant purpose. He may use someone's story of conquered pain to bring healing and freedom to someone else. No experience is a wasted experience with God. He redeems what was meant to harm us or defeat us and use it to bless us and others in the process.

Our stories have the potential to inspire out of their own pits of life. So often what we are trying to hide in our stories, God is trying to use. His desire is to use His story in our story to impact a world that is suffering. He chooses to use our weaknesses and brokenness as a platform for Him to stand on and declare to a world that no one is so broken that they cannot be made whole. God will use the jail-cell circumstances of our lives to reveal and produce His plans for our lives.

No doubt, without prison I would not be who I am and where I am today. I believe God used the path of prison to develop my faith and trust in Him. I am still on this journey of learning to trust Him more. I am still learning how to become who He created me to be, and I am enjoying this journey of self-discovery.

I am not the same person who walked into a cold Virginia prison, broken and hollow. I embrace the person I have become and the one who I am becoming. I have accepted the path before me. The path is not promised to be a road of ease and comfort. It may have some unexpected turns ahead and roads filled with debris. Yet, God doesn't often call us to the easy; He calls us to destiny. We will never regret saying yes to the path God has for us.

I believe God doesn't light the path all the way to destiny for us because if we saw the difficulties that we will face along the way, we would boycott the journey and forfeit our purpose in the process. When we allow trials and adversities to cause us to forfeit the journey, not only do we miss God's greatness for our lives but also the fulfillment of allowing adversity to shape and develop us for the destiny He has for us.

I used to wish for a different childhood experience, like those of my friends. They had family meals, family outings, and no abuse. But exactly what I wished to be different is exactly what God would use to birth my purpose. Sometimes our purpose is found buried deep within our pain. If we are willing to face and embrace the pain, even the scars that comes along with it, we can find healing and meaning beyond the scars.

I used to not want to talk about my scars because I was so ashamed. But now I understand that each scar tells a story of grace. This grace story says that God loves us regardless of our past circumstances or present realities. His love is even deep enough to dig us out of pits we dug for ourselves. Isn't it amazing that God's love will come after us and get us out of situations we put ourselves in? His loving mercy can even shield us from the consequences of our own actions.

I look back at all the things I've done that could have destroyed my life, but God's mercy shielded me from what my own actions deserved. Even in the things that were done to me, I see God's grace affording me the strength to overcome so that my story could one day inspire others to know that they too can overcome. Today I don't hide my scars, but I reveal them in hopes that they will bring hope to someone who feels insignificant like I once felt.

In my early years of prison, I used to think that years of my life were being wasted behind concrete walls and metal prison bars, but I've come to realize that no season is a wasted season when you come out better. Some valleys and dark experiences of life are necessary to build character, perseverance, and preparation for what lies ahead. My prison experience, no matter how dark, was God's tool of healing, development, and preparation in my life.

Prison prepared me for many things—including the day I would meet my biological father for the first time. I don't recall having face-to-face contact with my father while I was growing up. I know he visited once when I was an elementary-aged girl, but the only blurred memory I have from that visit were the gold necklaces around his neck.

A clear memory that I do have of my father was when I was a teenager and my sister was on a long-distance phone call with him while she was sitting in my room. During that phone call, I could hear him ask how she was doing and how my brother was doing. When he got to me, he could not remember my name, so he said to my sister, "and what's the other little one name again?" That day I closed the chapter to any desire to be reunited with my father. All these years, I was thinking, maybe one day we would have a father and daughter relationship. But that day, I shut those desires down.

But during my time in prison I made a conscious decision to forgive my father and move forward. God would arrange it so that in 2013, while my sister and I were preparing for a missions trip to Jamaica, we were informed through Facebook that our father heard we would be in Jamaica and wanted to meet with us. We told our mother, and she said we should see him. My mother never spoke negatively about my father to her children. She felt we needed to come to our own conclusion concerning him.

As my sister and I waited at the hotel for my father to arrive, I didn't feel much—no sadness, no happiness, no anticipation. I only felt like I was waiting for a long overdue appointment. I was surprised to meet a man who seemed shy and unprepared, conversationally. I immediately noticed that I have his eyes, and I also realized how much my brother looks and walks just like him. My brother's likeness to him saddened me because my brother has had a very difficult life, mentally. I wondered if things could have been different for my brother if he had a father figure to help him process his early teenage years.

As I sat across from a man who happened to be my father, I had a lot of questions running through my mind. *Did you care that there were nights we went to sleep hungry when we were kids? How did you sleep at night knowing you had three kids that you did not give any basic care?*

Some questions I did ask. These questions were not aimed to hurt but were asked for the sake of closure. He didn't have much to say. Our time wasn't long together. What *was* long was the almost forty years of silence from him. Before he stood to leave, he asked me for money. It was a sad moment. I was hoping for something more. In the end, I gave him all the cash I had on me, and that was the last time I saw my father. I never told my mother the details of that day, and she never asked. There wasn't much to tell except that I got the closure I needed.

Years before that meeting, I had learned to live without an "I'm sorry," and that day didn't change that reality for me. After that encounter I was at peace, knowing I felt no regrets or resentment toward my father. Who he was and who he chose not to be for the three children he fathered with my mother was a decision only he could reconcile within himself. Sadly, he passed away a few years after that meeting at sixty-four years of age.

I can't change where I've been or what has happened to me, but I can choose not to allow those things to dictate who I become. I made a decision to stop being a victim. I did this by letting go of the hurt and all those who hurt me, and by doing so I found peace. All along I was praying for peace, and I was the one holding it back by nursing secret pain. When I gave myself the freedom to feel the pain of life's challenges and yet move on in spite of them, I started to experience freedom—layers of it.

I rest my identity on the fact that God chose me before I chose Him. He chose me, knowing my faults and flaws. He chose me, knowing all the bad decisions I would make. He chose me, knowing I would doubt Him and display a lack of faith and trust in Him. He chose me, knowing I would give into temptations even though I possess the power to overcome them. He chose me, knowing I would often resist His leading and guidance in my life. But He also chose me, knowing He had plans to transform me, restore me, and put His Spirit in me. He chose me, knowing He would anoint me, empower me, equip me, and use my life as a platform to reveal His grace.

He chooses you too. The act of God's choosing of you and me, tell of a greater story; that God can choose and use anyone. He can choose and use the broken, the disenchanted, the used, the abused, the outcast, and the rejected, the educated, as well as the uneducated. It doesn't matter who you are, where you've been, or what you've done. God desires to use the unworthy to show us that our worth does not come from what we do or what has been done to us. Instead, our worth comes from Him and what He has already done for us.

When we look beyond the shadows of God's choosing, we find that His choosing is never about us as much as it is about Him—a God who chooses what many, even we ourselves, have rejected. I am so grateful He sees in us what we often do not see in ourselves: purpose!

Maybe you are reading this book thinking it is too late for you to walk in your God-given destiny. Perhaps you are thinking of the pain and injustice you have experienced that you just can't seem to overcome. Let me tell you that God still chooses you right where you are. He has a plan for you. You do not have to remain a victim to life's circumstances.

In God's providence, He can work in your life to orchestrate your destiny and your divine purpose. He is able to bring about a greater good from your disappointments, frustrations, and injustices. He desires to replace your ashes with His love...to turn around your adversities and restore your dignity.

God will overrule your past failures and inadequacies, causing you to soar beyond your deepest pain. Today, choose to square shoulders with that trauma, abuse, rejection, fear, doubt, or pain and say, "Today I have decided to be an overcomer. I choose to no longer be defined or held captive by the circumstances of life—past or present. Instead, I embrace the divine plan and destiny that God has for me."

There is one thing I know is true in my life and in your life: God will use difficult circumstances, disappointments, setbacks, and even pain to get us exactly where we are supposed to be, living out our purpose. Even in our darkest hour He can lead us to purpose. But we must give Him access. The moment I did, my life shifted direction for the better, and yours will too!

In the book of Genesis, Joseph did not know how his situation would turn out. We can read it in one sitting, but this was a life that he was living out over the years. I'm sure Joseph wasn't pursuing Pharoah's palace. What he was pursuing was God. In the pit he pursued God. As a slave he pursued God. And even in prison, he pursued God. No matter his adversity in life, he kept his eyes on God by walking in step by step obedience to God. He believed God had a purpose for his life even when the circumstances of life didn't look like it. God had a purpose for Joseph's life even while Joseph was in the struggles of life. This goes to prove that circumstances of life do not trump

God's purpose for our lives. He uses circumstances to impact our purpose and even propel it. You may want God to change the circumstance now, but God wants to meet you in it and use it as a platform to develop you for what he has prepared for you. We all want to live a life full of purpose and destiny, but sometimes the place where purpose is found and birthed is in our darkest hour.

*So, she looked back over her life and saw*
*God's hands of guidance through it all and*
*thought, "It was good; it was very good!"*

*You intended to harm me, but God intended it for*
*good to accomplish what is now being done...*

(GENESIS 50:20, NIV)

Made in the USA
Monee, IL
24 April 2024

57257081R00100